IS GOD EMERITUS?

OTHER BOOKS BY SHAILER MATHEWS

HISTORICAL

Select Mediaeval Documents
The French Revolution, 1789–1815
New Testament Times in Palestine
The Spiritual Interpretation of History
The Validity of American Ideals
The Making of Tomorrow
The Messianic Hope in the New Testament

SOCIAL ASPECTS OF CHRISTIANITY

Jesus on Social Institutions
The Social Gospel
The Individual and the Social Gospel
The Church and the Changing Order
Christianity and Social Process
Creative Christianity
Patriotism and Religion

RELIGIOUS BELIEF

The Growth of the Idea of God
The Atonement and the Social Process
Immortality and the Cosmic Process
The Gospel and the Modern Man
The Faith of Modernism
Contributions of Science to Religion
  With Thirteen Scientists
The Church and the Christian
A Dictionary of Religion and Ethics
  With G. B. Smith
A Constructive Life of Christ
  With E. D. Burton
The Student's Gospels
  With E. J. Goodspeed

New Faith For Old: An Autobiography

Is God Emeritus?

BT
101
.M46

BY

SHAILER MATHEWS

New York

THE MACMILLAN COMPANY

1940

First Printing

PRINTED IN THE UNITED STATES OF AMERICA
BY THE VAIL-BALLOU PRESS, INC., BINGHAMTON, N. Y.

FOREWORD

In this volume I have carried forward the line of thought of my *Growth of the Idea of God*. Its title might be regarded as an example of how personal experience gives rise to religious patterns! In my opinion, the critical changes through which the world is passing have shown the inefficiency of conceptions of God formulated in social conditions which have passed. The churches, as representatives of God, have been more concerned to prepare men for a post-mortem world about which they know nothing with certainty than for the organization of life in social, economic, and political conditions which they judged outside the realm of religion. The inefficiency of such a conception of God is seen in the tragedies of today.

If religion is to be any more than a palliative in the midst of struggle, it must be founded in that which lies outside of history. For some, dialectic metaphysics furnishes such a basis. For others, among whom I would be counted, the basis of religion must lie in cosmic realities which can be discovered by scientific methods. Naturally, such a conviction must share in the tentative attitude of science, but it cannot exclude from its interpretation of reality human individuals and social processes. They certainly are as real as what we call natural forces. Any philosophy of religion that will minister to faith must have as its outcome intelligent moral adventure. So long as it is believed that God stays in his heaven, all will not be right with the world.

I wish to thank the editors of the *American Scholar* and the *Forum*, the *Harvard University Press* and the *University of Chicago Press* for permission to use, somewhat rewritten, portions of material which they have published.

S<small>HAILER</small> M<small>ATHEWS</small>

The University of Chicago
August 1, 1940

CONTENTS

vii

technique of adjustment to personality-producing activities seen in evolution. Such activities still operative in the production of personality. VI. In religion such adjustment is personal, in science, impersonal. VII. The significance of anthropomorphism as a technique of establishing personal relations. Definition of God as an anthropomorphic conception of those personality-producing activities of the universe with which humanity is organically united. The reciprocity of adjustment to such activities. VIII. Such a definition of God excludes atheism. Cosmic activities are more than anthropomorphic patterns in which they are conceived.

The avoidance of difficulties arising from giving existential meaning to patterns does not forbid prayer. I. Prayer a utilization of the technique of human personal relations for the setting up of adjustments with cosmic activities. Prayer and communion. II. Prayer as adjustment to cosmic activities does not expect miracles. III. Such adjustment not identical with motive for prayer. IV. Immortality as dependent upon proper adjustment with cosmic activity. V. The church as a medium of adjustment to cosmic activity. VI. Summary.

The conventional conception of the will of God. I. The will of God as identified with a religion. II. Punishment as the result of the disobedience of the will of God. III. Morality as action in accordance with the personality-producing activities of the universe. IV. Significance of anthropomorphic conception of the will of God as love. V. The family as an expression of the cosmic activity. VI. The morality

of economic relations dependent upon the furtherance
of personal value. VII. Nations as possible cooperators
in the furtherance of personality.

IS GOD EMERITUS?

Chapter I

IS GOD EMERITUS?

When, thanks to the schoolmen, Aristotle became a minister of orthodox theism he introduced a new god to Christians. The philosophers treated the God of the Bible as in earlier times he had been treated by herdsmen and warriors. He became different. He would be an ingenious explorer who could find the conqueror of Canaan, Jehovah of Hosts, "in the Trinity of the divine persons discerned by purified minds." In fact, the term "God" historically viewed, has never maintained the same content. It has always been relative to the conditions under which those who used it lived. The Olympians and the Indian gods, Isis and Jehovah, were not creatures of metaphysics but of religion. They had reality as they helped adjust human life to the activities of the universe. As individuals they never existed. The God of orthodox Christianity has had great influence as a sovereign, but when metaphysicians have undertaken to prove his existence they have abandoned sovereignty and have turned to abstract or highly generalized terms. That is the element of truth which lies in the epigram that man created God in his own image. If God is only the imagination of the worshipper, the epigram triumphs. For the maker of epigrams, God, like Great Pan, is dead.

I

But obviously there are those who do not believe he is dead. Millions of persons worship him in thousands of buildings consecrated to him. Scientists write books about him. Children learn the Ten Commandments which he gave to Moses. Governors issue proclamations asking citizens to beseech him to regulate drought or rain as the crops demand. Prayer for his blessing opens public dinners and presidents call on their nation to thank him for whatever light may be breaking through the darkness of depression. Pacifists pray to him for peace, and dictators question his Nordic qualifications.

But if not dead is he *emeritus?* Is religion akin to the loyalty of old graduates to men who once were their teachers but who now have honor without classrooms? Are churches transcendentalized alumni associations?

If one were to listen to some of those claiming to represent the modern spirit, the answer would be a sophisticated affirmative. According to them, God reigns in the underworld of history, but has no place in the modern world of honesty, science and capitalism. Thanks to inherited religious attitudes, they may prefer to lament a departed theism rather than proclaim atheism but the emancipated see no future for the God of Abraham, Isaac and Jacob. He is the creation and symbol of ancestral piety and mid-Victorian wishful thinking.

Members of our intelligentsia mean to be polite to the God that they believe has retired from active control of the world. They may not pray, but they are not averse to church weddings and rather want religious color given to funerals. But, in their minds, God has really no duties to perform. He has retired into the Heaven of poetry and primitivity.

It is not hard to understand such relegation of God to innocuous desuetude. The God whom men have worshipped has not been the god of the philosopher. One does not pray to the Absolute or to Infinite Being or to an Other. The god of childhood can hardly be the god of the scientifically minded. The god of orthodoxy seems ill at ease in a universe of law.

In times of war come tragical doubts. How can a heavenly Father endure the destruction of millions of his children and the prostitution of natural forces he has created to an increase of human suffering? Why is he so indifferent to prayers for peace? Why does he permit war?

It would be a simple explanation for the insensate cruelty of men to deny the existence of God. But such a cutting of the Gordian knot of confusion and apprehension is prevented by the ineradicable conviction that God exists. Religious faith raises its own questions. If God is omnipotent and good, why does he let evil persist? If he is good but not omnipotent, what significance does he have? Why trust a good-natured but impotent deity? Is it not easier to say that he has withdrawn from the attempt to direct incorrigible fools?

Yet if we are to judge from philosophical and scientific literature, and indeed, from current fiction, even the most sophisticated feel that the world would be much better off if God could be induced once more to assume direction of affairs.

If there were not a God, Voltaire once said, we should have to invent one. That is a pragmatic argument which those possessed of privilege accept. Religion keeps the masses in order. The gods have always been friendly to the social and intellectual *status quo*. Socrates was executed as an atheist because he believed that the deity was more than the gods and goddesses of the Athenian state. Critics of our contemporary morals see chaos threatened if men cease to fear God's punishment for violation of the social code. There is little danger of revolution so long as religious authority is unquestioned. Even business men declare that spirituality is necessary if prosperity is to return, if banks are to lend money again, and the dangers of inflation are to be avoided. It may seem unfair to blame a retired God for the difficulties into which the economic order has fallen, but there is a general feeling that things will not be better until God acts. He must end his retirement. Do not colleges appoint elderly alumni as *interim* presidents while they search for young administrators?

II

It is not difficult to understand these inconsistencies in the attitudes of our supposedly intelligent class. The idea of God of one generation is an inheritance from its ancestors. In consequence, a religious faith has to be defended when the world-views of two generations come into conflict. And here we meet a basic fact in the history of the idea of God. In moments of distress and danger, men accustomed to accepting their fate from an absolute monarch found it easy to submit to an inscrutable providence. Their sovereign god might not be able to abolish evil, but he at least permitted it and would rectify all injustice after death. Belief in such a god was a source of courage and consolation to its possessors. It fitted into their world view. The will of God sent men on crusades, led them to accept earthquakes and storms and pestilence as punishment for sins, strengthened them to meet misfortune, and rewarded them for martyrdom and death in battle. His commandments were the basis of morality. His decrees fixed human destiny, and his acts, though inscrutable, were patterned after the justice and mercy of absolute monarchs. In a word, religion was of the same pattern as the pre-scientific, pre-constitutional social order.

So long as there is no radical change in a social order, religious thought can be pictured in the habits of actual human society. But when the mind-set of a group is modified, authoritative orthodoxy is, so to speak, left suspended in the heavens. Just as the gods represent outgrown social controls, so the patterns of religious thought no longer represent those of contemporary thinking. New tensions arise. Religious patterns suffer the same fate as religious practices. They may be respected, but they no longer represent actual intellectual life. They have to be defended by appeal to an authority which increasingly fails to represent controlling social experience. Patterns of religious thinking which once were identical with those of group thinking become vestigial because of new group practices. They are not born of the creative forces of new social conditions. Inevitably, therefore, they fail to minister to intellectual needs and a religion becomes in both practice and thought a sort of ghost of a previous social order. God acts in ways and his representatives think in patterns which are no longer those of the contemporary social order. Religion inevitably grows ineffective. God must be either left with the unintelligent or the pattern in which he is conceived must be changed. For only as a religious pattern aids in personal adjustment to forces in the cosmos is it really helpful. Man is no more passive in religion than in any other phase of life.

These phenomena are seen in the growth of the idea of

God in that highly developed religion, Christianity. The conception of God has grown as a social order has evolved a new social psychology.

Orthodoxy is transcendentalized politics in which a subject humanity has no rights, is born condemned to eternal punishment because of the disobedience of its first parent to divine command, and its supreme prayer to its divine sovereign is for mercy. Men have no power to do right except in the case of those who have been chosen by God to enjoy the pardon of their sins and have been given by him the ability to choose the right.

The rise of constitutional monarchy and democracy made such a political pattern derived from absolute monarchy inappropriate for religious thinking. One had either to accept it on the basis of some authority (that is, become orthodox) or re-think Christianity in patterns derived from creative social trends. The great mass of Christian people preferred to hold to doctrines which they had agreed to accept as supernaturally delivered, but a considerable minority endeavored to find harmony between a Christian faith and their social experience. And thus liberalism in the modern sense of the word was born. It was the expression in theology of incipient democracy. God, like the constitutional monarch, was judged to have duties as well as rights; and humanity, like the new nations, was judged to have rights as well as duties. True, democracy has never become a theological pattern like the absolute monarchy of the seventeenth century. Apparently men have not yet trusted themselves to elect a god. But one fact is plain: God has been identified with the pattern which religion has used. Lack of confidence in this pattern-God is born of a struggle between two social minds, one authoritarian, holding its religious patterns su-

perior to social change, and the other endeavoring to express
the values of the Christian religion in patterns drawn from
its own freedom and self-direction in political relations.

III

Theological thought which is the outgrowth of the former
of these two social minds sets forth God as "the infinite and
perfect spirit in whom all things have their source, support,
and end." The Westminster Catechism, a notable champion
of theism, declares that God is "a spirit infinite, eternal, and
unchangeable in his being, wisdom, power, holiness, justice,
goodness, and truth." To use the terms of logic, "God" is
thus a species of "spirit," but *spirit* is a term which has all
but dropped out of the vocabulary of psychology and has
no very precise definition in philosophy. Probably its most
natural meaning is that of something immaterial possessed
of conscious self-direction. It is not strange that persons
dominated by the concept of natural law, social process, and
experimental science should feel that any being so defined
belongs to the past rather than to the present.

Such uncertainty as to theism finds strange supporters
among Christians. Under the influence of European pessimism, it retreats into a sanctified agnosticism. God is not to
be directly reached by humanity. Men must wait for crises
introduced by him. In them he alone will act. Between him
and humanity is revelation. The unknowable God is seen
through his Word. But the meaning of this term is difficult
to discover. It is neither an infallible Bible nor the Christ of
the ecumenical creeds. The Absolute Sovereign is euphe-
mized into the Transcendent or the Other. The outcome is
logical. God has no immediate share in the direction of humanity. History is the record of demoniac power too great

to be opposed by man and can be overcome only when
God chooses to act.

IV

There is a psychological basis for this relegation of God to
desuetude. Philosophy has little emotional appeal. Every religion illustrates how the substitution of a de-personalizing
concept for the intimacy of personal relations with a god
tends to diminish the sense of dependence on the part of
worshipers. Imagination which no longer thinks of God in
the patterns of humanity does not arouse emotions which accompany the experience which shaped those patterns. One
cannot pray to a principle for mercy, or expect it from a
god who no longer has the attributes of an absolute king.
It is hard to substitute morality for sacrifice and obedience
to cosmic law for ritual. Anthropomorphism easily grows
concrete in idolatry. Michelangelo's picture of God in the
Vatican frescoes as a puissant old man and his portrait of
Christ as the judge listening to his Mother's cry for mercy
in the Last Judgment evoke emotional response not to be
expected from a conception of God as cosmic reason or as
undefinable substance. It is not strange, therefore, that when
members of a religious group seek their satisfaction in some
metaphysical ultimate, their observance of religious practices sanctioned by a social order should become conventional. When such conformity to an inherited religious attitude is regarded as superstition, philosophy becomes the
content of religious faith and is sharply distinguished from
morality. The worship of gods becomes a social vestige independent of ultimate philosophical faith.

The difficulties which lie in a change in an intellectual cli-
mate are everywhere discernible whenever religious thought

comes under the influence of scientific method. The fervor of a religious attitude is cooled by a different way of thinking. Questions are proposed to theism which demand other than the answers given by mystical piety or the discussion of divine attributes. Most religious doubt arises from the fact that men try to live in two intellectual strata. Problems proposed by a knowledge of natural forces and social trends cannot be answered by the use of theistic patterns embodying outgrown scientific assumptions and political experience. God comes under investigation. Divine decrees are seen to be not of the same order as natural laws. The creators of Christian dogma had hardly an elementary knowledge of science. For them a miracle was not only a fact but an evidence of the existence of God. For those accustomed to the domestication of nature by engineers, a miracle is unthinkable. Exceptional facts, such persons believe, can be brought within the general scheme of things. They cannot believe that diseases or accidents are due to specific decisions on the part of an omnipotent personality. They fear bacteria rather than devils.

The earliest attempt to give answers to questions propounded by the scientific skepticism of the eighteenth century was that of deism. God was believed to exist but was relegated to the position of a First Cause who had created and set in motion a universe from which he had withdrawn. As scientific research became dominant, religion had to concern itself with something more radical than ecclesiastical heresies. The political patterns in which its faith in God was expressed no longer led to prayer and pious submission. The champions of scientific research were often loyal to the Christian church, but God did not enter their laboratories, nor was he discovered by their microscopes and telescopes.

For less ecclesiastically loyal persons, the ultimate became the Unknown. Agnosticism checked affirmations regarding his relations with the world. God became unnecessary. Long live technology!

v

Such, in effect, is the plea of humanism—that philosophical cave of Adullam in which many sorts of rebels find companionship. With the positive terms of humanism any historically minded person must sympathize; so also with its insistence that progress will depend on intelligent social engineering rather than on divine interposition. One can also sympathize with its impatience with those who would substitute piety for duty and make faith in God an alibi for their own inaction. But, is that the last word on the matter? We have a universe on our hands. In it we have to live and move and have our being. Our life depends upon proper adjustment with the environing activities discoverable in an evolutionary process. Whatever philosophical and scientific hypothesis we may adopt, personality-producing activities must still be within our cosmic environment. Evolutionary process furthering personal values is an evidence of their existence as truly as heat is an evidence of those activities with which the chemist and physicist deal. One set of activities may be temporarily better understood than another, but they are equally unescapable and discernible. Gods have become *emeriti* when they are identified with patterns which are outgrown and in consequence cease to arouse emotional response. But this is not the end of the matter. Theistic patterns must be properly interpreted. They are not realities, but ways of making real activities of the universe with which

men feel they are directly and indirectly in personal relations. These cosmic activities assuredly have not been retired. What is needed is some new pattern in which they can
be more clearly mediated to human thought and emotion.

Chapter II

SUBSTITUTE GODS

Those who, without resolving the meaning of theistic patterns, feel that God has no immediate control over human affairs naturally demand some form of compensation. Intellectually this may be the assertion that God is a creation of man's fear and imagination and, therefore, has no reality demanding attention in the world of affairs. There is enough truth in this to give it a certain philosophical respectability, but it leaves men still subject to their religious urge. Did not skeptical Julius Caesar carry a little image of some god in the folds of his toga? Mankind has been said to be incurably religious, but men are not always intelligently religious. Even when they feel that the gods have retired, they do not like to proclaim themselves atheists. They become amateur idolators. Whatever god men may have on Sunday or profess in their creeds, for practical purposes they manufacture a god who will justify some line of conduct which they desire to follow. As the classical world relegated its great gods to a remote Olympus but placated the half-gods nearer home, these modern idolators make some useful practice or institution an ultimate court of appeal in their own conduct.

Of course we do not make idols in a literal sense. True, we have Billikins, but Billikins are not idols! True, we do not really believe in mascots—but how should we ever hope to win any conflict, from football to politics, without a mascot? True, we dislike to sit thirteen at table, but this is from the regard of the feelings of some one of the thirteen! True, we dislike to say that we are prosperous or that our children are well, without touching wood. But these customs are not idolatrous—they are only silly.

On second thought they are worse than silly. Each is evidence that men are ready to act as if the universe were not rationally ordered. And whenever a man substitutes chance for reason, luck for purpose, and a gambler's odds for definite planning, he makes a god of Chance, and Mischance rules him.

Most persons are above this insanity of trusting to chance. They make a god out of what is of great value in themselves —things of the utmost utility in life as we live it. That is to say, they make them the court of final appeal in moral action.

I

There is business, for example. No man would belittle its worth. The great monuments of our civilization are due to commerce. Our arts, our sciences, and our splendid institutions—these are all the blossoming-forth of the capacity of men to get wealth. Yet one can clearly see that when a person erects business into a court of final appeal in matters of morals he is manufacturing a god to get permission to do the things which he hesitates to approve. When a man says that this or that principle is not applicable to business in face of the fact that his Christian conscience tells him it is right, he is making a god to justify himself. A successful businessman once said to me, "I am just as much interested in ideal things as you are, but in my business it is not always possible to do the ideal thing." What is this but saying that business has been erected into a god?

II

Then there is the god of Social Convention. Social conventions are admirable necessities. How should we live the social life if not for these conventions? By them we know how many cards to leave when making a call, when to make our calls, what time our friends may reasonably be expected to wish to receive a call. What should we do without the countless other customs of life? They are the lubricants of our social machinery.

But we cannot safely make social convention the court of final moral appeal. Many customs do not tally with our ideals. We go shamefacedly to places of amusement, read certain books, wear strange fashions in clothes, dance suggestive dances. Everybody does it, why should not we? "Everybody does it"—as if custom made everything right! Children array themselves against their parents' advice, believing that what everybody wants to do is right. Men and women violate their best impulses and plead the same justification.

But no one ever erects that sort of god and elects to worship him without finding his moral idealism growing weaker. There is no god whose worship is more debilitating than the god—"Everybody does it."

III

We make a god of Culture. Far be it from anybody to belittle culture. To be able to appreciate real music as over against ragtime; to love real pictures rather than the vulgarities of the comic supplement; to appreciate real literature instead of the inanities of much popular fiction; to see that life is full of the laws of beauty and to enter into sympathy with those laws; to have fellowship with that which is true and beautiful and of good repute—these are some of the gifts of true culture. The mere ability to do the conventional thing is not necessarily culture. Learning is not culture. Some of the most learned people have manners for which one has to apologize.

But to honor culture may be to fashion one of the idols of our modern world. For it may spring from the distrust of moral standards.

I was once discussing the relation of art and morality with a well-known actor-manager. He insisted that there was no relation between the two, that a good (note the adjective) play could be written on any subject. "Do you mean to say that you can write a good play on the subject of a garbage can?" He was a trifle dismayed, but true to his logic, declared that it could be done.

Vulgarity often comes to us so alluringly through charming music, delicate literary style, exquisite artistic technique, that we are in danger of becoming artistically and technically skilled instead of being morally virile. Experience ought to convince us that this means moral decay. A soul who begins to substitute interest in culture for interest in moral life, is a soul erecting a new sort of god who will permit him to act, think, enjoy and ultimately believe that which is dissociated from personal values. For in the case of culture as in that of business and social convention, we do not create gods to make morals sterner.

IV

Sometimes we manufacture a god out of the noblest and most precious material—Social Service. Far be it from anyone to speak a word except of heartfelt admiration for that new attitude of scientific helpfulness which marks our age. But to make social service an expression of religion is one thing; to make it a substitute for God is another. So to love the heavenly Father as to practice fraternity with earthly brothers—that is the heart of the ethics of Jesus. But to hold that there is no immorality, no right or wrong; that life has nothing but universal misery; and that in this service of misery one has the only possible God, is the heart of an altruistic pessimism.

Those who practice it remind one of the nobles during the French Revolution, as they mounted the tumbril with women and children. They wiped the eyes of the little children and cheered the women to die bravely. But they were all on the way to the guillotine. They were fellow-victims, without hope of rescue.

There is no enthusiasm in forlorn hopes. You cannot worship one whom you pity. You cannot make social enthusiasm contagious if you feel that the world is not worth saving. Social technique should be a servant rather than a master.

V

Then there is Nationalism. It is getting to be conventional among idealists to treat nationalism as something to be avoided. Humanity, we are told, is more than a nation. That is true, but any impartial study of history shows that the development of the nations led to most significant changes. From a world broken into innumerable feudal fiefs, where there was practically no court of appeal except military power, when the castle rather than the courthouse was the symbol of authority, there emerged our modern nations. Sovereignty became a basis of political unity, and law was enforced upon individuals whose rights were increasingly recognized. Whatever may be the ultimate relationship of human beings in the world, the nation has been a source of economic and social progress. Patriotism and citizenship are more than rhetorical terms. To salute the flag is more than a convention.

But nationalism as a court of final appeal in morals is more than a name for collective activity. It may be an excuse for dispossessing individuals of their rights and making the state the supreme end. So long as personal values are thus subordinated to a political program, religion as a social factor must either be suppressed or relegated to the field of piety and preparation for life after death. Nationalism becomes a god without love and justice.

VI

Doubtless those who thus unintentionally become idolators would say they believe in God. But they do not think of him as immediately concerned with their affairs. He is to be worshiped, but not obeyed. He will save them from hell, but is indifferent to the morals involved in sharing in the life of some group. Religion becomes an appeasement program in which the rights of the individual are sacrificed to immediate needs.

In this creation of substitute gods we see the perversion of religion. It is more than the effort to define or picture deity. Men want to justify their action by recourse to something more ultimate than the action itself. The difficulty with such idolatry is that it is morally disintegrating. Long years ago a Hebrew prophet condemned idolatry in words applicable to that of our day. Of the man who made a god of a piece of wood useful for various domestic purposes, he said, "He cannot tell that he has a lie in his right hand." There must be something more final than efficiency. Mythology and poetry have their place in the realm of religion, for they presuppose realities which are more than themselves. But to submit to gods born of a rationalization of what is contrary to recognized moral ideals is worse than worshiping idols of wood and stone. They, at least, suggest that which is more than human.

Chapter III

GOD AND COSMIC PROCESS

What faith can one hold when the God of outgrown patterns of thought no longer helps? A really religious person needs more than aesthetic enjoyment. The grandeur of cathedrals, the inspiration of sacred music and the appeal of ritual may quiet but will not satisfy a longing for God or help one to find order in the confusion of our day. Our natures find peace only in the discovery of meaning in the processes in which we are involved. But where shall such a sense of meaning be found?

If the testimony of the ages is to be trusted, it will be found in God. But what, our day demands, is this God? No sublimated sovereignty, no mechanistic unity, no abstract principle, no unknowable and unapproachable Being will suffice. God must represent activity that is beyond doubt or definition.

I

Peace of mind, which is more than blank submission to fate or chance or any other ultimate, has been found in what is claimed to be a revelation of God. In undeveloped religions such revelation may be some natural object or event which breeds terror or furnishes joy. In more developed religions it is the inspired teacher who reveals mysteries ordinary men accept but do not understand. In many religions revelation comes through the ecstasies and visions of one around whom followers gather. In the Christian religion revelation through seers, prophets, and Savior appears in the literature of the Bible. For millions, the Scriptures have become an authoritative revelation of God which has been expounded and expanded by the dogmas and rites of Christian churches.

But at what stage does inherited religious experience become sufficiently authoritative to satisfy human needs? Perhaps it is safest to answer: when the revelation embodies what is regarded as the supreme element in the life of its believers. Therein is relativity. Certainly the man of our day would not regard as ultimate the God who inspired Samson. Only when re-interpreted can an inherited revelation answer the intellectual queries or calm the momentary fears of successive ages. The creeds of Christendom, the Confessions of the Protestant state churches, the romantic theology of unmethodical liberalism contain no absolute revelation of God. They are all relative to the social orders in which they appeared. Even if one grants that a church has the power to add to the revelation that it has inherited, the difficulty is not removed; for in this supplementary revelation current culture, current political theory, current scientific conclusions make the idea of God progressive and in retrospect tentative.

There is naturally a feeling of security when once a claim to revelation is accepted as final and not subject to inquiry. But such security exists only as one yields to authority. Such authority has lain for centuries in a formula like the Nicene Creed. It has to be accepted in order to be discussed. Yet if, so to speak, the natural history of a creed is investigated, its authority weakens. For those who accept an authority that

forbids investigation, theism becomes a postulate which men
may explore and defend but must not seek to explain or
even to understand.

Yet even in the case of an authoritatively revealed God
such as is contained in the Christian doctrine of the Trinity,
there is a recognition of something more than dogma. Theological treatises set forth arguments for the existence of God
which are not based on revelation but on philosophy. The
evidences of intelligibility and trends in nature supplement
revelation. Indeed, by a logical *tour de force* they are held to
defend revelation. But in so doing, the Trinitarian conception disappears, except as dogma to be accepted. When a
theologian, for example, is asked to distinguish between the
personae of the Trinity, the differences become hardly more
than terminology. The Father is unbegotten, the Son is be-
gotten, and the Holy Spirit proceeds. But logic must go one
step further. Since the *personae* are of one substance and are
involved in the definition of that substance, then all of them
are in each. The divine substance cannot express itself par-
tially. The Father and the Holy Spirit are in the Son, the
Spirit and the Son are in the Father, and the Father and the
Son are in the Spirit, since each is of the substance. The doctrine of the Trinity thus shapes a metaphysical conception
of Deity known in three different relations. It is this Deity,
rather than the revealed Trinity which the philosophical
argument for theism seeks to establish. In so doing it moves
away from revelation to a consideration of the universe.

II

Nor does everyone find satisfaction in some metaphysical
abstraction. The God whom men worship is not the principle
of integration, the totality of good in the world, the universe

in its ideal-forming capacity, the conservation of values. Such definitions may serve as a basis for a philosophy of religion, but, except for the acutely philosophical mind, they are too abstract to be a basis of conduct. Even Thomas Aquinas would hold that in our earthly life the effects of God's action rather than his essence are to be seen. But how can one be sure that they are such effects? Philosophers have never absolutely established the existence of God. The arguments for theism have substantiated faith already existent. It is only when men have sought to account for morality or immortality, or to gain courage in the midst of the vicissitudes of life, that the so-called ontological, cosmological and teleological arguments have made their appeal. Religion is more than intellectual probability. Metaphysical formulas, as truly as revelation, derive the content given the word God from the experience of those who have sought divine aid. Metaphysical definitions of God, however abstract, imply analogies as truly as poetry and religious ritual. For it is the way of language to be symbolical. However one may quiet intellectual doubts by philosophy, for practical purposes religion will find its emotional power in that which is concretely rather than abstractly pictured. To capitalize abstract terms does not create a personality. To distinguish between transcendence and immanence assumes a dualism in the universe which has never been metaphysically determined. The God of metaphysics as truly as the God of theological revelation is a projection of a faith which is grounded not in the intellect but in the urge of life.

III

There is a third way to religious and moral assurance. It is to discover what reality the word *God* represents which is more than the patterns drawn from social behavior. And that way lies in an understanding of man's relation with the universe.

We may as well face frankly the fact that such a method will not be approved by theologians. It opens up the conflict between science and theology. Nor will it be approved by neo-Thomist philosophers. It opens up the question as to the relative importance of facts and philosophy. The revival of interest in Thomas Aquinas involves the question as to whether facts furnish their own basis of generalization, or whether they must be treated as intellectual Helots serving material needs but incapable of contributing to the spiritual wants of humanity. And even below this is the question as to whether facts discovered by scientific procedure are the helots of an infinite Being distinct from nature. Thus the intelligibility of nature, the possibility of organizing natural laws, contribute to the argument of design for the existence of a God distinct from nature. Facts are the effects of his work, but in themselves have no significance comparable with metaphysical exposition.

But such a revival of scholasticism ignores the fact that most of the data of modern science were not in the possession of the school-men. One cannot help speculating whether Thomas Aquinas could have been as satisfied with Aristotle if he had known of Darwin, or whether Augustine could have been so confident of original sin if he had been acquainted with modern biology. The paucity of knowledge led them to dialectic procedure. Cosmic activities were too little known to interfere with the conviction that there were realities corresponding to words and that their relations could be determined by the logical relations of such words. The validity of a major premise could never be checked except by appeal to authority or a new syllogism. It followed that, while such methods of thought were penetrative and often salutary, the value of facts was lessened as compared with generalizations which had not been developed by inductive processes.

It was inevitable that conceptions of God as a personality distinct from nature should have used the pattern of the soul or spirit as distinct from the body. Theism could appropriate the evidences of natural law as indications of the way in which this infinite personality worked, but it rested upon a dualism which assumed rather than tested such an analogy. It is at this point that most attacks on theism have been made. For it could well be questioned whether the facts mustered for the existence of a Reason apart from the universe might not apply as well to aspects of cosmic activity itself. Such a question cannot be answered by appeal to authority. There must be understanding of the data which scientific experimentation has disclosed.

Atheism has made the same assumption as that of scholasticism, namely, that God is an ontological term. As such it is no longer needed for understanding the universe. The struggle between scholasticism and atheism is really a struggle between two methods of understanding reality which have the same metaphysical definition of God.

Without such definition, let us look positively at the facts which scientific investigation both in the field of nature and social process put at our disposal.

IV

It is unsafe for one who is not an expert in natural science to use scientific discovery precipitately. But it is no more precipitate to be hypothetically constructive than it is to be dogmatically destructive.

In modern physics matter is something very different from what it seems to be in everyday experience. In our conventional way of thinking, matter is something solid and dead. To the physicist it is activity. According to one view, matter is impelled by force; to the other, activity constitutes matter. If matter be composed of undulations in a hypothetical ether, it has less solidity than an old-fashioned ghost. Even a semblance of solidity disappears. We are left with no analogy save that of activity in thought and will, while to the physicist the ultimate formula of matter is a mathematical equation.

At the same time we know enough as to how this unknown and indescribable ultimate operates to have our textbooks on physics and chemistry and physiology. But each science is only departmentalized knowledge of some aspects of this infinite activity from which all existences have emerged. The electrons, protons, atoms, molecules, colloids, and organisms are all combinations of the same ultimates reacting to different activities of an environing cosmos. The striking thing about such a sequence is that as the combinations grow more complicated they develop more freedom and self-direction. Their latest form is the personal individual.

Any world view which attempts to embody a fact such as this is subject to limitations. We find it hard to divorce the idea of solidity and deadness from our concept of what is called material. It is misleading, therefore, to use the word "materialism," even though we give a new definition of matter as activity. To speak of monism or panpsychism or even idealism in the Berkeleyan sense is also misleading. Perhaps our best word is "activism" for such a world view. We instinctively read into other terms concepts born of a prescientific conception of the cosmos. And because of a similar danger that we use a machine as a pattern, we do not use mechanistic terms like force, power or energy.

Cosmic activity is something like the hyperbola. We do not know whence it comes nor whither it goes, but within the area of observation it is possible to discover specific tendencies. Agnosticism as regards their origins is no basis for denial of the stages of a discernible process. Physicists do not tell us what electricity is, nor biologists what life is, but their agnosticism as to the ultimate nature of things does not prevent the study of activities which are attributable to the unknown ultimate. If we do not know what electricity is, we can at least turn on the electric light; and if we do not know what life is, we can satisfy our hunger.

Within this area of observed cosmic activity is evolution. This is a word neither to be juggled with, nor absolutely defined. It is rather a symbol of observed trends within the cosmic activity. It would be presumptuous to claim knowledge of the universe as a whole, but one line of process is certainly discernible, and that is the evolution of personality.

It has sometimes been charged that those who accept evolution as a basic interpretation of history float "blissfully down the stream of contemporary civilization, confident of the divinity, yea, the Christlikeness, of its prevailing currents and the happiness of the condition towards which it is tending." But certainly such a characterization is not accurate. Theological liberals do not believe in evolution as an impersonal force which can be trusted to bring about a better world automatically. They certainly are not so simple-minded as that. Process is not identical with progress, for it may be devolution. But whoever accepts the findings of science as to the genetic relations which explain a sometimes imperfectly traced process, gains a new perception of religion as something more than an inheritance of ancestral fears.

V

The starting point for any understanding of religion must be humanity rather than revelation or metaphysical formulas. Among the various forms of human behavior there has everywhere been an attempt to derive help or protection from those forces upon which men have felt themselves dependent. These methods have varied with different civilizations and have usually been of two sorts. One is that by which the conditioning elements of an environment have been treated personally; and the other has been the attempt to control these forces by some impersonal coercion. The first sort of behavior is that which the word religion represents, and the second that which is commonly known as magic. It is difficult to distinguish between the two, for there is an area within which the personal and the impersonal are indistinguishable. One method may appropriate elements of the other. As a civilization becomes more complicated, the distinction becomes more pronounced, and eventually becomes that between religion and science. For the understanding of the human behavior which we classify as religion one must keep this distinction in mind. To describe religion as the quest of the good life is to ignore the differences between the two types of activity. Each seeks the goods of life in its own way.

Such a distinction, however, does not argue that an intelligent religion must not use the facts given by science. It is true that the methods of science are not those of religion, but no religious faith can be satisfactory that is out of harmony with what have been shown to be the facts of the universe. A theism that would satisfy an inquirer whose starting point was a pre-supposed revelation, fails to satisfy those who have shared in the scientific knowledge of the last century. It is not that theologians have been indifferent to the science of their age, but that such science has become obsolete. It was only natural that when their theism was carried by Christianity into the age of science, it should have found itself in a struggle with new knowledge.

Two postulates given by this new knowledge underlie any attempt to understand the religious activity. The first is that religion is an extension of the biological fact that life is conditioned by an organism's adjustment with and appropriation of elements within its environment. The second is that cosmic activity is the environment with which life must thus be related. Both of these two postulates are indispensable if one is to understand a religion. What separates religion from science is that in the former adjustment is made on the level of personality. As an outcome of evolution a human being as a living organism must not only maintain, like all animals, a proper relationship with chemical elements and physical forces, but it must also set up relations with those activities of the universe which have made personality possible. It is this new aspect of life which separates the human from the sub-human elements of the cosmic process. That there are such personality-producing activities in the universe is clear from the fact that out from the ever-increasing complexity of the combination of cosmic elements, personality has emerged. And those activities are still within the environment with which life must be adjusted. Otherwise the human organism would revert to the animal or, as in the case of death, to that which we ordinarily call impersonal. A water-breathing animal that becomes an air-breathing animal demonstrates the existence of air. Without it, it would perish. Since it does not perish, the air must exist. An animal which has become personal would likewise lose its characteristics if there were not activities in the universe with which it can live personally.

But the biological analogy must be supplemented by an analogy to be found in social relations. By them a human individual is made personal. Without them he would be simply an individual. Such relationship is within the area of experience. Social environment sets the conditions in which individual persons are in mutually responsive relations. The danger of extending mechanical conceptions into such a relationship has been repeatedly emphasized by the representatives of the social sciences. But we are so accustomed to dealing with machines and impersonal forces that the temptation to conceive of personal relations mechanically is always with us. When we speak of the personality-producing activities of the universe we are not thinking of a distinguishable force like that of electricity but of that recognizable process in which the potencies of ultimate reality find expression in trends which, at least on our earth, emerge in human beings. Such a personality-producing trend is an expression of a cosmic totality discernible in successive stages in its development. The emergence of human personality from the cosmos presupposes other stages in which it is potentially but not actually present.

VI

To speak of personality-producing activities of the universe is not to say either that the universe itself is personal or that there is an individual person existing within the universe. Relationship of the kind we call personal does not wait upon such metaphysical decision. In this relation religious activity is akin to scientific experiment. To no small degree it is tentative and experimental. We can discover and better understand forces with which we can cooperate and which we can appropriate. We know the conditions under which an organism maintains its individual existence. When those conditions are not met, we know that the organism disintegrates and is said to be dead. We are increasingly acquainted with certain forces which the term electricity represents, and we know the conditions under which these forces can be utilized for different ends. While we may not know the ultimate nature of those activities which constitute our universe, we do know how to adjust ourselves to them and can perceive the conditions under which they can be made helpful, as well as those under which they are harmful.

One indispensable prerequisite of such reciprocal adjustment with a cosmic activity is that it be consistent with the organism. We do not attempt to set an icicle on fire or turn an electric switch to sprinkle our lawns. The same is true in the case of religion. As we come to know the activities of the universe, we find the conditions under which we can cooperate with its personality-producing activities. Where the knowledge of natural forces is incomplete, the ways of cooperating with them may be naive or even mistaken. But there will always be the experience of the race which makes some sort of adjustment possible. Otherwise the race itself would have disappeared. Increase of knowledge will give increase of helpful adjustments, as is shown by our domestication of physical forces in the interest of more enjoyable living. All this is true of that cooperation with the universe which we call religion. Its methods must be of the nature of the relationship. We cannot be religious impersonally. If an organism is to survive it must preserve that adjustment with cosmic activities which gave it existence. If the adjustment and the response are in the area of personality, the methods by which they are realized must themselves be personal.

Increased knowledge, both of the environment and human nature, will determine the limits and the technique within which this personal adjustment takes place. Such increase in knowledge may be expected to make more effective the adjustment. Certainly the better knowledge of human nature given by psychology and the social sciences may well replace methods based on pre-scientific beliefs. It is, for example, one thing for a religion to expect occasional visits from supernatural beings living in a geographical heaven arching above the earth, and quite another thing for a religion to use knowledge of astronomical and physical facts. But in both cases the attempt to set up a help-gaining personal relationship with activities of the universe persists, even though the gods may have been consigned to mythologies and museums.

Religion is the reciprocal personal relationship of humanity with those personality-producing activities of its cosmic environment with which it is organically related. Although obviously such a conclusion leads to speculation as to the ultimate nature of being, it does not rest upon metaphysics but on data given by science, and particularly upon the recognition of human life as a disclosed trend within a total process. The necessity of personal adjustment to elements of the total environment is as imperative as mankind's adjustment to other cosmic activities. Each religion is a technique for such adjustment.

VII

In their religions men have found in their social experience techniques for adjustment with cosmic activities. Anthropomorphism is not confined to religion. Do we not speak of Mother Nature? And is not a nation symbolized as John Bull or Uncle Sam? And is not a college Alma Mater? Even the language of physics, when it is not strictly mathematical, is as analogical as that of theology. Human experience is the basis of all description. There would be no knowledge of our friends and neighbors without anthropomorphism. Because we know ourselves as personal, we believe that personality is expressed in those purely physical experiences by which we know each other.

A human body that is seen, heard, and touched is no less material than a wax image, but we attribute to it qualities we find in ourselves. Thereupon we set up personal adjustment with it. The universe is no more material than are our bodies. Anthropomorphism can be extended to it by experiment and understanding. Certainly, such extension as an attempt to come into dynamic relationship with a conditioning environment is justified by the intelligibility and traceable trends which a growing knowledge of the universe discloses. Such knowledge may forbid our use of the naive anthropomorphism of the ancient religions, but it does not forbid adjustment with the universe on the level of personality by the use of personal experiences. The history of

humanity is no more the history of impersonal relationship
with the universe than it is that of successive attempts to
make personal adjustments.

We have already seen how anthropomorphism has appeared in the Christian religion. It is not difficult to trace the
development of the Hebrew monotheism as seen in the Old
Testament record. The conception of Yahweh was expanded
as the Hebrew people's social and political life developed.
The God of a nomadic tribe became the God of an agricul-
tural community and, as the Hebrew nation became monar-
chical and involved in international relations, Yahweh became the sole God of the universe. Yet he always maintained
a distinct personality possessed of the qualities which were
regarded as morally supreme. It was never necessary for his
worshipers to discover some metaphysical entity lying back
of his activity as the philosophers and religious teachers of
Hellenism found metaphysical monotheism lying back of
their gods and goddesses. His actions were those known in
human relations. Yahweh was the creator of the universe
so far as it was known by Hebrew teachers, the director of
national policy, the punisher of national disloyalty, and the
hope of a world order in which his law would be observed
and happiness assured. This faith was inherited by the Christian church and expanded into a cosmic sovereignty whose
pattern was set by the political development of western
Europe. Then the infinite sovereign, philosophically defined,
retired into theology. The operating religion of Christians
was less that of a worship of an infinite spirit and more appeals to the Virgin Mary and innumerable saints. Such practices were never treated as idolatry but rather as means by
which God could be emotionally approached. It was natural,
therefore, that there should come a cleavage between this

popular religion and the philosophical theology of the clergy.

When the content of the word *God* is examined, as has already been noted, it is seen to be relative to the social process. The concept, the vocabulary, and the practical exposition of the meaning of the term have always been a more or less refined anthropomorphism. The rites and the theology of the church, as truly as the practices of the masses of the people, were means by which men won the favor and the help of a God who could be described anthropomorphically but was believed to be greater than words could express. The history of Christianity, as well as of every religion, thus makes it plain that, while the term *God* was assumed to imply a personal existence, *it was in reality an anthropomorphic conception of those personality-producing activities of the universe with which humanity is organically united.*

For those who thus recognize the term as interpretative rather than ontological, the pattern is not that of politics but of biology. As an organism seeks the development of life through relationship with an environment which has conditioned its development, so men seek relationship with the cosmic activities on which they more or less intelligently find themselves dependent. If the flower in the crannied wall is to picture what these relations are, it must be left in the crannied wall. The reality of relationship is destroyed by analysis. We do not seek to prove the existence of an undefinable God but the legitimacy and efficiency of theistic anthropomorphism in establishing help-gaining relationships with the personality-producing activities of the universe.

Such a reciprocal relationship may be seen in friendship. Friendship is a mutual relationship of well-wishing. If one were to use academic language, friendship is a term of mutual relations in which the subject and the object are both active and express the same attitude. That is what makes a friend more than an acquaintance.

If God be the concept which expresses cosmic relationship with man and man's relation with the cosmic activities on the level of personality, obviously it expresses the response of those activities. This, as already pointed out, is involved in the biological pattern of the relations of humanity to its environing activity. The term *God*, therefore, while not in itself existential, expresses a reality and a relationship which are not imaginary. The anthropomorphic term, "Uncle Sam," for instance, represents a geographical, biological, and social reality with which individual citizens are related. But just as truly "Uncle Sam" represents activities which affect those individuals. Without such symbolism the term would have no more meaning than a term like *chimera*.

When men speak of God they naturally attribute to a concept of relationship qualities which are derived from human individuals and officials. Properly understood, the term *God* projects cosmic reciprocity on the level of personality. By it the personality-furthering process is recognized as responsive to, and furthering the development of personal values through humanity. To attribute familiar personal activity to such cosmic response is not to create a metaphysical entity but to indicate a relationship which furthers the process from which human persons have emerged. In so doing it becomes an element in a total reality of cosmic adjustment.

From such a point of view, God is not emeritus. The term becomes an instrumental concept by which is furthered that reciprocal adjustment with cosmic activities which it is the aim of every religion to establish. Its efficiency depends upon the content given it by the ideals which it embodies.

All religions are expressions of this sense of organic unity with that upon which humanity as personal seems to be dependent. The mystic has no monopoly of such relationship. The church that limits grace to those who have met certain ritual and theological conditions has a technique of adjustment just as truly. The man who sees in brotherhood a personal adjustment with the coordinating (or nucleating, or integrating, as one prefers) activity of the universe has it also. All alike recognize their personal relations with cosmic activities which they did not originate, but from which they sprang and with which they must be in harmony.

VIII

The natural objection to such a view is that this is not the sort of God men worship. They want a Sovereign or a Father who holds his children's hands and in other respects is a transcendentalized parent. In answer to prayer they want him to cure sickness, ward off danger, and arrange the weather to suit their needs. But when did men ever worship the god of philosophy? Only when the Absolute has been personalized by capital letters or poetry has it been the object of prayer. Pluralism, with its finite god, may be a romantic interlude in theological thought, but sooner or later one has to adopt a realistic view of man's relation with the universe. As a matter of unemotionalized fact, our ideas of God are shaped in patterns which rationalize cosmic urge inherent in life itself. Human beings can no more abandon their trust on that which is believed to be cosmic than they can abandon breathing. The patterns with which they picture and justify such recognition will vary from touching wood to belief that the universe is instinct with activities with which one can be personally adjusted. But, whether intelligent or unintelligent, whether superstitious or philosophical, men seek help from that upon which they feel themselves dependent and over which they have no control. When they do this by impersonal techniques, they are scientific. When they do it by utilizing personal experience, they are religious.

Atheism is excluded by such judgment. The use of the term God is a recognition of the fact that our patterns are aids to actual adjustment to reality. It does, indeed, prevent the belief that cosmic activity can be treated as if it were an infinite human individual. To give existential meaning to such terms as father or sovereign is to revivify a theism that is no longer efficient. But it is legitimate to use such terms as aids to the realization of the fact that cosmic activities from which personality has evolved are not mechanistic. Like all terms aiding the establishment of personal relations, God is a symbol of an actual reality. In calling someone a friend we are not discussing physiology, but we know that without physiological reality friendship would be impossible. So with the term God. The universe given us by science is presupposed by religious behavior. The possibility of expressing its activity in mathematical formulae justifies the conviction that human personality can find within it response akin to itself. That indeed is implied by the interplay of organism and environment in the evolution of human beings. In fact, many who treat the term as existential shrink from speaking of God as a personality. They prefer to say that God can be spoken of as personal in that his actions are *like* those of human personality. Such an analogy involves a dualism in which the universe is distinct from God. More realistic is the interpretation of the universe itself as infinite activity in which human personality has emerged, and of God as a conception born of personal experience with human persons by which the adjustment of humanity with cosmic personality-producing activity is furthered.

Chapter IV

PERSONAL ADJUSTMENT TO COSMIC ACTIVITY

Religion has its psychology, but it is more than psychological. This will appear if we attempt to summarize our line of thought. The various theories as to how one experiences God are all anthropomorphic. In conventional religious behavior the habits and emotional responses of human relations become the patterns of relationship with a postulated ontological deity. Sometimes such behavior becomes the extremely emotional and, it must be added, sometimes psychopathic experiences of the mediaeval mystic. Since the language of many of these celibate mystics is erotic, psychologists account for their ecstasy as a sublimation of sex. By the less mystical believer God is called upon to help in any sort of human need. In many cases prayer is a demand for miracles. When failure attends human effort, God is called upon to do that which men have been unable to do. The experience of childhood is elevated into a faith in a Father. Distressed souls find confidence in the thought of divine love, and anxious souls find security in the divine will. In the peace which follows such faith there is found an evidence of the working of a divine person whose ways are past finding out but whose will can be trusted as righteous. Misfortune and sorrow are the discipline of a loving Father.

However such faith may be disturbed by questions as to

how an omnipotent good God can permit evil, it is basically sound. The abandonment of conventional ideas of a personal God does not forbid legitimate religious experience. So long as we live in a universe where personality-producing activities are operative, religious experience is more than the operations of glands and emotions. We are the outcome and are organically connected with that which is cosmic. Religious experience represents a definite relationship to that which is objective to ourselves. Just what the ultimate nature of that relationship may be we do not know, but, so far as our own personalities are concerned, we, like all living organisms, are affected by the environment which demands personal response to personality-furthering activity. No organism can be uninfluenced by the environment upon which it is dependent. The anthropomorphism which is fundamental in all personal relations is an agent by which the reciprocal relationship between the human person and the personality-producing activities of the universe is made real and established. Conditioned as this anthropomorphism must be by our increasing knowledge of the self and the universe, it is legitimate. Personal experience on the human plane can be used to appropriate cosmic influences. That is the supreme service of the concept of God.

I

Prayer is a universal element in religions. According to the intellectual development of a social order, it ranges from the elemental cry for help in meeting life's needs to the conscious search for moral strength. In its form prayer will always be born of the practices and attitudes with which human beings seek to set up personal relations with each other. The urge to get satisfying relations with the personality producing activities of the cosmos will use the instrument of such fellowship with one's fellow men, that is to say, conversation. For those who think of God as a punitive sovereign, prayer will consist of cries for forgiveness and mercy and laudation which characterize all rituals. For those who are freed from such elemental social attitudes, prayer may be a personal approach through words or unexpressed thoughts to those activities upon which life depends for its personal values.

Prayer establishes a personal relationship peculiarly sensitive to cosmic response. Whether this be the emotional ecstasy occasionally enjoyed by the mystic, or the peace and new moral strength which commonly attend prayer, the relationship is more than subjective. One might call it bio-mysticism, the interrelationship of a personal organism with that environment upon which it depends. This relationship in the realm of personal adjustment cannot be described in impersonal mechanistic terms. The anthropomorphic pattern is imperative. We cannot speak of ourselves as cogs in a machine or of the environment with which we seek personal adjustment as impersonal force. The relationship is one of mutual response on the level of personality. But intelligent prayer will not be contrary to what we know are natural forces. Jesus would not tempt God by defying the law of gravitation. Our growing knowledge of the universe and of natural processes sets limits within which prayer can be offered. We may pray for what we want, whether it be our daily bread or the establishment of international peace, but the value of prayer will not be measured by miracle.

And yet, the analogy of life's adjustment to responsive environment does not forbid the belief that prayer may have effects other than in the experience of the individual. Certainly socialized prayer in worship furthers the group appropriation of cosmic activity and serves to establish conditions which otherwise would not have existed. The operation of cosmic activity is always affected by techniques. We reach new efficiency in ordinary affairs by proper adjustment with electricity, light, gravitation, and heat. While such forces operated before scientists developed the techniques, after such development the operations of such material forces are conditioned by new techniques. It is certainly not to force the analogy to say that in the intelligent adjustment of our fellowship with the personality-producing activities of the universe there should follow results which otherwise would be lacking. Intelligent religious exercises are not a form of defeatism or wishful thinking. They indeed indicate a desire for divine assistance, but they are no more irrational than methods of utilizing those forces to which we give scientific names like electricity and gravitation.

Such adjustment has sometimes been described as communion with God. The psychological value of such religious exercise is undeniable. The saints of all religions have practiced it. It is, however, not exactly the same as prayer because it is passive rather than active. It is more meditation than cooperation with cosmic activity in the furthering of personal values. There is in it a tendency to withdraw from the world of affairs. Such spiritual exercises, however, are valuable for the development of spiritual strength as an accompaniment of prayer. They are valuable as they stimulate sensitiveness to impressions of the cosmic from which prayer results. It is significant that Jesus has

no provision for such spiritual exercise. It belongs rather to
a religious attitude which distinguishes what it calls spirituality from morality. The great Christian mystics have never
been content to treat the experience of meditation as final.
It became a reinforcement for service to their fellow men.
In healthy minds the peace and emotional uplift which
come from the contemplation of spiritual realities within
the Christian religion lead to renewed determination to extend personal values in social relations. In such undertak-
ings prayer leads not to withdrawal from human life and
the enjoyment of spiritual solitariness but to an extension
of the personality-producing activity through human personality. Meditation which accompanies such moral activity
is concerned with methods of conduct.

II

It is necessary to distinguish sharply between prayer as
a means of inducing God to meet some specific demand
and prayer as a helpful relationship with the personality-
producing activities of the universe. Prayer as ordinarily
practiced undertakes to get superhuman action even in the
realm of morals. Men pray God to keep them day by day
without sin, they ask him to grant them grace which will
enable them to do his will. In more specific demands God
is asked to cure the sick, end war, care for the poor, and
save men from danger by the immediate interposition of
his power. Organized religious groups use prayer as a
means of deriving all forms of special help. The psycholo-
gist must determine how far the faith which prompts such
prayers is accountable for what the believer and the ecclesi-
astic regard as divine answers. One cannot overlook the

innumerable cases in which prayer for health has been cur-
ative and prayer for guidance has resulted in clearer insight
and fortunate decisions in business. But such facts are offset
by failure to gain blessings. Unanswered prayers are so
numerous as to give rise to a religious philosophy declaring
that God does not grant requests because men ask amiss, or
he wishes to discipline those whom he loves. A balance is
thus struck between the granted and the denied requests.
In all cases the will of God is done.

But there is a deeper philosophy of prayer than this. The
effort to induce divine interposition in human affairs is an
expression of personal adjustment to cosmic activities. It is
this adjustment that is important, however unintelligent
or even impossible may be the request. It is not magic, but
the instinctive expression of life. The attitude of prayer,
rather than answer to prayer, is the essential element.

Cooperation with personality-producing cosmic activities
may not lead to that quietism which accepts the will of a
heavenly father or a heavenly sovereign without complaint,
but it stimulates cooperation in creating new personal
values. The Stoic might accept nature and submit, but the
intelligently religious man sees in evil the lack of reciprocity with cosmic activities and therefore is stirred to new
action. He preserves his own personal integrity and endeavors to organize life in such a way that the personality
of others is recognized and developed. The ideal life ceases
to be one of submission, and the peace which passes understanding becomes that of an experimenter. He is less concerned with thoughts about God as a personality, and more
with individual and social adjustment to cosmic activity.
Religious thought may become tentative, but religious action becomes confident. Situations which repress personal

values are sin—opposition to cosmic process. Endeavor to
rectify them can count upon the cooperation of that process.

Such an intelligent faith will find itself enriched by
poetry and art. Its vocabulary may abound in the words of
childhood. Efforts of a father to further the personal development of his children may help him to think of a heavenly
Father. Submission to law and observance of the power of
the state may serve as an analogy for his conformity with
cosmic activity. But the terms will none the less be analogies. Corollaries which suggest new difficulties in religious
faith cannot be drawn from them. Prayer will be a medium
of adjustment through personal living. Faith in an orderly
universe and participation in its development of personality
will give courage and sacrificial social-mindedness in efforts to make a society moral.

III

There is what might be called a sinister aspect of prayer
as an attempt to utilize cosmic activity. Its limits are clearly
set. It must be in the direction of personal values. Otherwise prayer is opposed to the very nature of things. It is
akin to black magic. Psychologically it may give efficiency,
but it is the efficiency of rebellion. Sooner or later it will
bring suffering.

This is not to say that professed motives determine the
cosmic adjustment. That is no more true in the case of
prayer than in the case of unintended or unconscious adjustment to physical forces. Here is the simple question:
is that which the soul desires in accord with the activities
making towards personal value? Man did not originate
those activities. One may act in ignorance. Indeed, one's

conscious motives might even be opposed to them. But, as the Psalmist long ago said: "God makes the wrath of man to praise Him." One is no more free from cosmic law in prayer than in the use of fire. Relationship with the evolutionary thrust through humanity has its results, whatever prayer is offered. If such relationship is in accordance with the personality-producing activities, there is progress. If such relationship is sought as a means of accomplishing anti-personal outcomes, it furthers such maladjustment as assures suffering.

IV

From this point of view immortality becomes something more than wishful thinking. It is true that the vast majority of men and women have shrunk from annihilation, but it is hardly enough to say that immortality is probable because men long for it. Men long for health but sooner or later fall victim to disease and death. The crude hopes which make future life the continuance of the earthly have always been discounted by philosophers, and the descriptions of theologians are metaphors expressing the assurance of future happiness. We are really forced back upon the question whether the continuance of the personality after death is tenable in view of our knowledge of the conditions of life. Certainly the old argument of Socrates and many others that the soul existed before birth without a body and therefore exists after death without a body will not find many supporters. It is to answer one difficult question by raising another which is even more difficult. If we lived in a dead universe or a static universe or a universe that had not produced human personality, the question of immortality could never arise. But such a universe would be one in which there is no humanity.

The line of development which our various sciences enable us to trace can be understood only on the assumption that the various combinations of matter are influenced by new adjustments to elements within the cosmic environment. The crystal responds to heat and light, the vital to those elements in the cosmos which make life possible, and the personal to those cosmic activities which have made personality possible. For, if there is to be any form of existence capable of personal life, it must be adjusted to the environing cosmic activities upon which it is dependent. That there are such activities the existence of ourselves as persons demonstrates. The law of evolution is that some additional and creative cooperation has occurred between the organism and previously uncorrelated elements of the cosmic environment. The relation of persons to the conditioning activities of the universe may therefore be regarded as promising still further development of personality. Otherwise such cosmic activities, as well as our relations with them, must be regarded as having become static. I cannot see that in the choice between these two alternative hypotheses there can be any hesitation. The universe as infinite creative activity has not become extinct. The process must go on in the field of personality as it has gone on in the lower levels. The potential possibilities which have thus been gradually accumulating in the evolutionary process will, as men conform to the personality-producing activities of the cosmos, emerge in still further organized personality. The part realizes new possibilities in its relations with the whole.

This is, of course, another way of stating what is commonly called the religious argument for immortality. But it has this difference: God is not thought of as an entity objective to the universe imparting grace, or as immanent in dead matter, or as an undefined spiritual order over against nature. The conception of the soul as an independent entity in space is replaced by a concept of an evolutionary product developing new personal characteristics by new appropriation of the personality-producing activities of the environing universe. The cosmic trend towards production of personality would thus be carried forward by the development of new combinations within the human individual which are superior to the conditions set by those physiological inheritances that produce death.

This means, of course, that immortality is no more a matter of religion than is birth or the structure of the universe. If we are immortal, or if we become immortal, it will not be because we want to but because in a universe like ours we can no more help it than we can help feeling warm before a fire.

v

Individual religion has an experimental laboratory in social relations. From an evolutionary point of view, society becomes an element in the environment in which the individual must live. An individual becomes personal as he shares in the interplay of other individuals. That is to say, the evolutionary process, which is really a form of cooperation of elements, finds renewed expression on the human level. Through social grouping a new relationship is established to cosmic activity. If such social action furthers the development of personality, it gains the support of the personality-producing activities of its environment; and if it makes impersonal or anti-personal ends supreme, it is in opposition to such activities and must suffer the outcome which always follows when an organism becomes maladjusted to the environment upon which its existence depends. It has too often been the case that the search for the knowledge of God has neglected this elemental fact. The disciplines of solitariness have centered in an individual's salvation.

It is natural that a religion should be the expression of a group interest, whether that be, as in the more primitive religions, a total community or, as in the Christian religion, a church. No society can prosper except as some type of mutuality is embodied in its customs. The group, if free, tends to increase personal values, but if it recognizes caste or slavery or racial inferiority, if it depends upon terror, its violation of the cosmic activity checks social process and the extension of personal value to individuals.

Because of this law of social development, a church is important as an agent of religion. It becomes a point of contact with the personality-producing activities of the universe. Any social group has a significance which is more than the sum of the influence of the individuals of which it is composed. These individuals are affected by a group consciousness and influences which otherwise would be lacking. While it is true that a group tends to grow rigid as it becomes organized, and ecclesiasticism may dull the interest in the personal development of individuals, it is none the less true that within a religious community there are ideals and customs which conserve such personal values as have resulted from social organization. However one may be compelled to criticize the limitations of a religious group, and however its leadership may yield to the pressure of political expediency, it is none the less true that churches become channels of cosmic influence. As an atom carries electricity, a religious group carries those activities of the universe to which the evolution of personality is due and upon proper adjustment with which the growth of personality depends.

Ritual, religious assemblies, the organization of group beliefs contribute to the social expression of religious attitudes. In their origin they spring from some customary action or belief. It is only when, because of such customs, ecclesiastical procedure is believed to have an independent efficiency that its inheritances further religious inertia. But such a danger may be overestimated. When through social action words or acts become symbolical, they may further religious experience, just as the saluting of the flag may express and conserve national loyalty. One can unite with others in religious worship with this understanding. Creeds, rites, hymns, forms of worship are conventional expressions of faith which might require very different expression if treated as matters of fact. In this regard, participation in conventional religious practices is not hypocrisy. It is like participation in social conventions. One can shake hands with a friend without raising the question as to whether one is thus protected against the weapon which otherwise might be drawn. Despite its origin, the handshake represents friendship. So, too, religious practices. In sharing in them one shares in a socialized attitude which they represent. To repeat creeds which represent this group solidarity is not hypocrisy when one recognizes that he is thus continuing an attitude which the group conserves without attempting to revise its expression. In the course of time a church consigns such inherited expressions of its attitude to symbolism, or quietly ignores them except as historical documents. As a conserver of these attitudes rather than of rigid dogmatism a church is an agent which furthers the individual's appropriation of the personality-producing activities of the universe.

VI

It may seem to some that such a presentation of the power of prayer is unsatisfactory. They have never examined critically the terms in which they address the deity. To them the idea of God is not instrumental but that of an undefined being whose actions can possibly be affected by petition. To such persons the thought of prayer as a mutually responsive relationship with cosmic activity will have little appeal. It may seem too abstract. Undoubtedly it is easier to pray to some intellectual image than to understand the reality which it represents. But after all, prayer as an expression of desire for divine help is not the same as a philosophy of prayer. To be childlike is not to be childish. To act as the child of a divine Father is to recognize that relationship which the parental analogy represents. It certainly excludes mechanistic dependence on impersonal forces. Our ignorance of the nature of our relations with the universe does not compel us to stifle the instinct to express our personal relationships with that which has made personality possible. An understanding of prayer as an expression of life obviously reaches beyond logical definition, but it is no more irrational than life itself.

But prayer is not the only way of cooperation with the personality-producing activities of the universe. Not all persons have the temperament which makes prayer natural in other moments than those of crisis. But the way of morality is open to all. Whether or not one prays continuously or occasionally, he must always act in such a way that this adjustment with activities furthering personal values is effective. That is what is meant by doing the will of God.

Chapter V

WHAT IS "THE WILL OF GOD"?

The conventional appeal to the will of God is usually paralleled and interpreted by the appeal to conscience and to revelation. But, as acquaintance with the history of morals will show, the deliverances of conscience and revelation are not always identical with wisdom. In many cases, what is called conscience is a combination of obstinacy, prejudice, and devotion to the *status quo*. Revelation as found in the sacred literatures and ecclesiastical decisions is said to be progressive. But this is equivalent to saying that its specific content is never absolute. Too often it is a formula which sanctifies selfish desire and resembles the profession of a warring nation that it seeks for a just peace. But as justice, in international as truly as in penal practice, is retributive, Christian theologians have stated that God may be merciful but he must be just, that is, punitive.

Such statements are admittedly only partial. The Christian religion confessedly honors sacrificial love rather than punishment as the will of God. But such social mindedness always involves some Calvary. It is easier to fight for rights than to give justice which involves an understanding of the conditions which have led men to violate the rights of others. And it is also true that the history of a civilization has been marked by a progressive ethicizing of what is regarded as the divine will. It has been difficult, however, to accept that will as absolute. Intercessory prayer and worship which is hardly more than flattery have been made a basis for hoping to induce an infinite sovereign to do what the worshiper believes ought to be his will. Both parties to a controversy wish divine assistance. Struggle on the battlefield is duplicated in the courts of heaven.

However inevitable and even helpful such anthropomorphism may be, it is limited to social ideals which are regarded as beyond question. That is one reason why so many intelligent persons feel that God is not trustworthy. He is too easily swayed by human appeal. The ideals for which his will stands may be granted, but there is no basis for believing that they have any sanction which guarantees their observance.

I

It is easy and in fact customary to identify the will of God with the tenets of a religion. A religion is not a force which, like electricity, operates independently of humanity. It is a social behavior that undertakes to gain what is regarded as divine assistance. It gets its power not simply from its doctrines and shibboleths but from the inertia born of social solidarity. It is only too plain that a religion may be a source of danger. The identification of the program adopted by a religious group with the will of God has repeatedly led to war and cruelty. Inherited religious prejudices identified with divine will have complicated the politics of more than one nation. The history of western Europe illustrates only too plainly how organized religious antipathies may lead to war. Religious groups have too often opposed the extension of rights and sanctified social injustice. Any religion which champions an outgrown *sta-*

tus quo as an expression of divine will becomes anti-social. As in the case of Russian ecclesiasticism, the will of God may be identified with a hostility to the extension of political rights and economic justice.

The power of a religion to increase human betterment and security is undeniable. But since it is a form of social behavior expressing a fundamental human urge, its beneficial influence depends upon an understanding of social process, sympathy with human needs, and the conviction that the conduct it sanctifies expresses something more than that which is merely opportune. Intelligent religious faith forwards the social life when men see that intolerance and selfishness cannot be sanctified because they are opposed to the personality-evolving activity which is in the very structure of the universe. In a varying degree such recognition is in the ideals of every developed religion but too often the latter is distorted by individual and social selfishness. To wait inactively for God to do that which demands human cooperation is moral cowardice. To feel that individuals, social classes, and nations can cooperate with cosmic activities is more than a championship of religious inheritance. Any description of the will of God which is less than cosmic may be a tool of the demagogue and the reactionary.

II

According to all religions disobedience to the will of a deity is followed by misfortune. In primitive religion, tabu is so universal as to be regarded by some anthropologists as the basis of religion. It would probably be more accurate to regard it as a religious technique on the level of primitive civilization. The mythology of the Aryan races abounds in tragedies resulting from the violation of the will of some god or goddess. In the Hebrew religion, the will of Yahweh, revealed in the various codes and the teachings of the prophets, is the center around which the history of the chosen people revolves. Disobedience brought punishment upon individuals and nation alike.

The will of god varies with the character of the god; it is what a community regards as proper social practice. God is revengeful where society regarded feud and revenge as social imperatives. The Yahweh of the time of the Judges not only approved but commanded the wholesale massacre of enemies. As the social ideals of the Hebrew people were enlarged by international relations and the religious philosophy of Egypt and the Mesopotamian valley, the will of Yahweh expressed the ideals of a developing civilization. Divine commands showed moral advance, but with the exception of some of the more far-sighted prophets they were concerned primarily with national rather than individual behavior. Socrates found the will of God in a supreme deity rather than in conventional worship of innumerable gods—and was executed as an atheist and an enemy of the state. Plato, moving from the concrete to the cosmic, made the will of God equivalent to pre-existent ideas. As the Christian religion developed, the will of God was expressed on the level of social practices and the elaborate dialectic of the Schoolmen, in the brutalities of the Crusades as well as in the mercy and sacrifice of St. Francis.

Whatever content has been given to it, the will of God has been regarded as that to which humanity must submit. The theology which rests upon revelation found in divine decrees the explanation for sin and salvation alike. Revelation of the divine control of nature and humanity gave

unity to thought. Thomas Aquinas in combining revelation
with Aristotelian dialectic did more than indulge in academic discussion. He made the will of God as known
through revelation the center for the educational and political life of a social order. But in so doing he perpetuated the
biblical inheritances. Back of his philosophy lies the belief
in a personal God who is distinct from the material universe and the humanity which he had created. The pattern
in which his control was exercised was that of idealized
sovereignty. The explanation for the forces of nature as
truly as the course of history was the will of an absolute
monarch possessed of omniscience, omnipresence, and holiness. As "essence" or "being," he could not be seen by physical apprehension but only by angels or disembodied spirits.
In the world of sense only the effects of his activity could
be perceived by men who were still living on the earth.
With the rise of scientific experimentation and the gradual
subjection of deductive to inductive thought it was inevitable that the decisions of this God who existed as an infinite person in the midst of the universe should give rise
to questions which could not be answered except by an
implicit faith in what a church had declared to be true.
The necessity of such implicit faith might be justified, but
it did not rest upon reason but on the admitted authority
of revelation as contained in the Bible and the decisions of
the church. As Protestantism abandoned, at least formally,
the authority of the Catholic Church, the schism between
science and theology became more pronounced. The so-
called Illumination in Catholic countries like France resulted in atheism. With the beginning of the 19th century
the break between scientific thought and reliance upon the
revealed will of a personal God was to some extent adjusted

both in the Catholic and Protestant apologetics. Evolution, as well as other disclosures of scientific procedure, was regarded as the way in which the God of revelation worked. But this resulted in still another schism between those who refused and those who accepted such compromise.

III

The absolute basis of morality, however imperfectly expressed in human history, is conformity with the personality-producing activities of the universe. That integrating activity which has made electrons into atoms, atoms into molecules, and molecules into organisms continues in humanity on the level of that which is personal. Such personal integration is love—a cosmic activity as truly as electricity. Nothing can be safely described as the will of God which ignores this fact. The misery that comes from war, the suffering which results from economic struggles, the cruelty of coerced idealism, the selfishness which would gain justice rather than democratize privilege are the outcome of the disregard of love as a cosmic activity. As gravitation will hold up a wall when it is plumb, but ruin it when it is out of plumb, so to disregard love as the integrating activity of the universe in the area of personality is to insure unhappiness. To act cooperatively for the welfare of those involved in the same situation is to cooperate with cosmic activities which are as real today as in the past. Love, therefore, becomes a practicable basis upon which to build human relations. It is the only will of God that is absolute. To rely on force rather than on the recognition of personal values is to revert to a pre-human mode of life.

Love is more than sentimentality or even affection. Just

as science undertakes to show us how to live with and get help from the forces of nature, so a religion must inspire people to discover the ways of such cooperation in establishing personal values as will be a projection of cosmic personality-producing activity. The more intelligently we further human values, the more are we in accordance with cosmic activities and carry forward the cosmic process in which we are involved. We have long been taught that sin is born of selfishness. We need to realize that selfishness is opposition to cosmic activity, possible because such opposition is in the area of the personal rather than the impersonal. Religion as impulse for personal adjustment with the personality-producing activities is implemented by knowledge of conditions in which such adjustment is possible. But such implementing must always recognize the supremacy of the personal. The history of humanity might be described as the record of the struggle to prevent the substitution of impersonal for personal ways of action. We are not yet wise enough to see that real progress in human affairs depends upon adjustment with cosmic activities making towards the personalizing of human individuals as economic efficiency depends upon intelligent cooperation with natural forces.

IV

Here one sees the importance of a correct anthropomorphic picture of our relationship with the cosmic activities. To portray God as fatherly does not read human self-consciousness into the universe but utilizes human experience in developing personal relationship with the cosmic activity which has made us personal. To speak of God as love is to recognize in such activity that which could not be expressed by the analogy of the machine or of force. Thus it becomes a basis for a morality which tests itself by personal standards. Such a test is unequivocal. It prevents self-deception in the choice of means and methods. It subordinates immediate good to ultimate good. Analogies in life are innumerable. Immediate advantage led to the unintelligent destruction of forests and the consequent erosion of tillable land. Immediate advantage led to the exhaustion of tillable land by unintelligent croppings of the soil.

The choice between courses of action must be determined by the simple test: which ultimately furthers personal values. Such a decision will rarely be unaffected by men's desires and ignorance. In too many cases, a perpetuation of the *status quo* will be judged as preferable to changes extending personal rights. Substitute gods may justify action opposed to cosmic activity which, through individuals possessed of the rights of persons, would make towards the better organization of social, political, and economic relations. Such action does not further personal values and will bring suffering. For it is a revolt against the universe. Religiously speaking, it is disobedience to the will of God.

v

Moralists of all times have struggled with the question of pleasure. They are practically agreed that pleasure cannot be an end in itself and that happiness as distinct from pleasure is the accompaniment of perfection, whatever that may mean. But abstract argument is less conclusive than the test which religious faith recognizes. The animal instincts are legitimate, but they are not exclusively human. They must be controlled and fitted into a perspective which includes the development of personal values rather than the enjoyment of sub-human animal desire.

The family as a social unit is an agent of such development. It is more than a device for the regulation of sex. It is a social projection of the creative activity which furthers personal values through combinations of less personal elements. The self-discipline which would make our animal inheritances conduce to personal values finds its basis in something more permanent than social convention. The moral relations of the sexes are grounded in this conviction that anything which tends towards the belittling of personal values is opposed to that which is ultimate in the universe in which we live.

VI

The same test must be applied to the economic relations of life. In no other sphere of human interest is more clearly seen the emergence of the struggle between the impersonal and personal interests. Mankind has had to depend upon nature for support. In the most primitive days the supplies of life were gained largely without labor through hunting. Then came the obligation of women to do work which the hunting and fighting male felt was below him. Slavery made it possible for women to limit their work to domestic services while slaves with few personal rights provided support for a family or tribe. As civilization developed, slavery was replaced by freemen or serfs whose rights of personal movement were limited. As the economic techniques developed, especially after the invention of machinery and the expansion of the capitalist system, there arose the struggle of the wage earner for the enjoyment of liberty, leisure, and larger participation in the product of his toil.

At the present time, the enlargement of such personal privileges directly and indirectly affects the social order in every part of the world. In the history of this development within social life, it is plain that the general line of progress has been towards the extension of privileges, formerly enjoyed exclusively by those who possessed power, to the underprivileged as human rights. True, the progress has been broken by the temporary triumphs of those who possessed means of coercing the underprivileged to accept their status. In too many cases, inequality of privilege has been sanctioned by religious organizations who saw the will of God in the perpetuation of the *status quo*. But there has been no reversion to slavery or serfdom. Even in totalitarian states there is a profession of regard for the welfare and happiness of individual citizens.

Such a progress sometimes has been explained in terms of economic struggle, but such a philosophy of history is too simple. Economic efficiency has never sufficed as an explanation for the furtherance of rights or the extension of social privilege. There are too many elements in the struggle which are not economic. The question will always arise why civilization and economic efficiency accompany the recognition of the rights of individuals, as our Declaration of Independence says, to life, liberty, and the pursuit of happiness. However limited and uneven the achievement of economic rights appears, the trend of human history makes plain that civilizations progress in the proportion as personal values are recognized in economic relations. That is precisely what would be expected if the constructive activities of the universe are themselves productive of personality. The methods proposed for the readjustment of economic life must, in the nature of the case, be experimental, but in the choice between them the decision must ultimately be reached by an estimate as to whether they conserve and advance personal values. Such choice cannot be determined simply by immediate efficiency. There must be intelligent decision as to whether in the long run readjustment is in accord with the personality-producing activity of a cosmic environment. Only then can it be said that economic efficiency expresses the will of God. Only then can it further human welfare.

In reaching such a decision it is obvious that social processes must be intelligently understood. Prejudice and passion are no substitute for wisdom. The scientific study of society and so-called economic laws is essential for determining whether a proposed change furthers the trend toward personal value. In such decision experimentation is as imperative as in the field of physical sciences, but it is far more complicated. The impersonal forces of the universe can be described in formulas derived from innumerable experiments with constant factors. Wherever humanity enters there is introduced the inconstancy born of the self-direction of persons. But human history is not a succession of accidents. Social trends can be valued in the light of human experience. A moral order is as discernible as the laws of the physical universe. Conformity to such order cannot be assumed in the case of personality as in the case of atoms but the alternative is absolute. In the same proportion as economic relations are in accordance with the personality-producing activities of the universe, human welfare is assured. In so far as they are opposed to such activity, suffering is inevitable. The human race, like

the Hebrew people, is always on Mount Gerizim and Ebal
choosing between the blessings which follow obedience and
the curses which follow disobedience to the will of a God
of love, man's interpretation of the personality-producing
activities of the universe.

VII

It is from this point of view that we look at the relation
of nations. We have been told that justice is a civic virtue
stopping at a frontier; that a nation is an end in itself; that
it is idle to speak of right and wrong when national action
is concerned. We might, we have been told, as well speak
of the right and wrong of biological law. A weak nation
has no rights which a strong nation must respect, and a
strong nation has rights which a weak nation must respect. For such a political philosophy national might is
national right.

It must be admitted that historical support for such denial of moral obligation to nations is not wanting. There
are few generations who have not been forced to endure
war. And war is a denial of the personal value of the individual. Even those who would not subscribe to the political
philosophy which makes national efficiency a justification
for ignoring liberties, racial equalities, and rights of mi-
norities, find themselves forced temporarily to adopt methods they abhor for the defense of their own national well-
being. Such reliance upon war is evidence that men have
not yet learned to think of a nation as a moral entity. The
only will of God that a warring nation desires to have done
is military victory. Yahweh of the Hosts was not a pacifist.
In the conquest of Canaan under his direction, the rights
of a nation to own the land on which they had developed

a civilization never troubled the invading Hebrews. Their God had given Canaan to them, and his will was that they should conquer it.

If this be the will of God, it is idle to think of international morality. If there is nothing better in the processes of social evolution than that of war sanctified by religious faith, the world of tomorrow will be built on the tragic precedents of today. If nations are to have no respect for the rights of other nations, civilization is only animalism prostituting science to destructiveness.

We need a higher moral estimate of nationality than is in evidence. We need not only to realize that nations exist for the personal welfare of their citizens but that as political units they must recognize each other's rights in the furtherance of such welfare. Isolation may bring temporary safety to a nation, but only in cooperation with other nations in furthering personal rights will a nation be at one with cosmic law. But the realization of this fact is possible only when a nation itself recognizes personal rights as the end for which it exists. International morality presupposes individual morality. It is idle to expect national altruism in a nation of selfish citizens. Until citizenship is sufficiently enlightened to see that love, that is, cooperation on a personal level, is a practicable basis upon which to build human relations, a state will be at the mercy of those who can control its military and economic resources. When the spirit of acquisitiveness dominates individuals, acquisitiveness will determine national policy. If a nation is to carry forward personality-producing processes, it is not enough for its citizens as individuals to do good to individuals of other nations. They must make a nation itself socially minded in its relation with other nations. Indi-

vidual morality must result in a social morality wider than
national frontiers. Patriotism must be made moral by international cooperation.

The sacrifices which such international morality involve
will be possible only when the citizens of a country are
convinced that it is really better to give justice than to
fight for privilege. This is a hard enough lesson for individuals to learn, and at the present time it seems all but impossible in the case of nations. But for those who realize the
possibilities of cooperation with the personality-producing
activities of the universe, it is a call to prophetic effort.
Morality is a product of cooperation between the members
of a group. That will be as true of nations as of individuals.
A God whose will does not extend to nations is no God of
internationalism. He becomes an enlarged tribal deity, and
his worshippers are less intelligent than those who use the
impersonal forces of the universe for the purpose of de-
stroying men and property.

If the progress of a nation is to depend upon the misery
of the rest of the world, if increase in employment and
emergence of prosperity are due to the development of war
industries, if its enjoyment of peace and freedom is born
of an incalculable expenditure for army, navy, and air-
planes, to speak of helping build national morality is close
to hypocrisy. Whether we realize it or not, our hesitancy
or readiness to be grateful to God for a well-being based
upon others' misfortune is a test of our religious intelligence and sincerity.

But there is another way of looking at national development. We can be legitimately grateful that prosperity,
peace, and security are conditioned by conformity with

that which is in the very structure of the universe. One can be grateful that he lives in a universe where selfishness does not have the same outcome as love, where happiness is more than animal pleasure, where evolutionary progress follows new recognition of men and women as persons.

From the point of view of this faith, we see that democracy is the process of democratizing privileges, rather than an ultimate static social order. What is more, we see that those who in the course of social evolution have gained privileges, cannot with safety either for themselves or for society treat such privileges as theirs exclusively. Privileges are not rights, but trusts for others; the advantages of the few which must become the advantages of all. To maintain any monopoly of privilege resulting from imperfect social adjustments runs counter to cosmic process. The Christian may, of course, reasonably question any proposed method by which socialization of privilege may be accomplished, but he cannot doubt that such extension of personal values is the one way of progress.

The sufferings which follow any other estimate of human values should convince us that we are not simply enjoying illegitimate wishful thinking. To develop freedom of thought and action, personal equality, and the recognition of an international cooperation is no easy task. But a nation that undertakes it is aided by those cosmic activities upon which personal welfare depends. Gratitude for any degree of success in such an undertaking is anything but hypocrisy. In religious terms it means the recognition of the fact that God works in social process. National well-being is more than accident. As we undertake to develop national life and the building of a world in which war will not be the final court of appeal, such a faith in cosmic cooperation gives courage to combat national and individual selfishness which would make a nation an agent of coercion rather than of cooperation.

Chapter VI

JESUS AND GOD

The central principle of a religion can be known by the symbols which it regards as sacred. When life itself becomes tabu so that the killing even of an insect is a sin, it is natural that sex should determine sacred images. Where unconscious being is the end towards which successive forms of life move, it is natural that life should have its compensation in god or goddess to whom prayer can be offered for each need. When God becomes so transcendent as to be isolated, it is natural that the images or paintings of beatified persons should be regarded as having power to help or hurt humanity. When an individual founds a religion and receives the worship of his followers, he acquires a superhuman significance as savior or prophet. In all such cases we see a dramatization of the tendency to bring an object of worship into the realm of sense. It is only when such a religious trend is undermined by new intellectual attitudes and economic change that sacred persons join the company of the emeriti.

Such general statements can be illustrated in any religion but in none more clearly than in Christianity. Its character can be seen in its symbols. The historical Jesus became the incarnation of the deity, and the loyalty and faith of his original followers became the worship of the Son of God, the second person in the Trinity. The records of his life have been reinterpreted in the light of the developing religion, and the messianic interpretation of primitive Christians has become a dogma of his deity.

It is easy for those who recognize the power of the psychology of a religious group to see in such facts only an illustration of the god-making process. Indeed, the history of Christianity is claimed to give color to such an interpretation. The dramatized anthropomorphism became metaphysical. Men pray to Jesus as they pray to God. The prayers to God the Father are in the name of his Son, conceived by the Holy Ghost, born of a virgin. Stated thus baldly, the dogma of the deity of Christ seems vestigial. Orthodox theology becomes its own disillusionment, and Christianity dissolves in a philosophy of religion.

But such an outcome is born of the overstatement and misinterpretation of the place of Jesus in a religious movement. A dogma is a formula protecting religious faith. However precisely a council or a religious body has expressed its belief, every dogma has been born to legitimatize intellectually a spiritual attitude. Christian theologians have never permitted their religion to become the system of philosophy by which it was defended. The sacraments show that Christians have felt that there are depths of religious experience which escape definition and require symbolical action.

Of no dogma is this truer than that of the metaphysical deity of Christ. No one can study the two centuries which preceded the Nicene Council without feeling that the discussion with which they were filled was not born of anxiety about mere words. The faith that in Jesus one could see the presence of God in an individual life was at stake. Assaulted on the one hand by a universal polytheism, and on the other by a philosophy drifting towards impersonalism, the developing Catholic Church felt that it was useless to speak of a Christian salvation unless deity had actually met and saved those who accepted Jesus Christ as Lord. Can anyone, however he may question the finality of the metaphysics which lie beneath the dogma, think of any defense of a religious faith more effective in the early Christian centuries? Even when the formulas of the councils have ceased to express the intellectual attitudes and social experience of later centuries, they have been sacraments in words through which men have confessed their participation in the continuous group of those having faith that in Jesus and his teachings God is mediated to human needs. This faith has always been greater than the formulas in which it has been expressed. Jesus is the symbol of a religion.

I

The only definition which can include the variations of the Christian movement is that Christianity is the religion of those who call themselves Christians.

That is more definite than it sounds, for men and women who have called themselves Christians have regarded Jesus as the author of their salvation. The formulas in which they express their loyalty to him are patterns as varied as the civilizations and groups in the midst of which they have lived. But genuine identity lies in the acceptance of Jesus as a means of setting up help-gaining relations with God and more personal relations among men.

At this point frankness is indispensable. Intelligent persons will not be satisfied with any attempt to resuscitate the first stage of Christianity. Modern Christianity is the descendant of the religion of the men who wrote the New Testament, but it is not identical with its ancestor. The first Christians were Jews; no one of them broke with the Jewish church. Their thought was conditioned by the institutions and the prevailing culture of their own times. Jesus was no more a philosopher than a legislator. He shared his contemporaries' belief in demons and the speedy end of the world. He attempted no reform of the state and taught his disciples to accept the *status quo* even to the point of suffering injustice. To apply his poetic aphorisms literally to our modern world is impracticable.

The same is true of Paul. He, too, believed in demons and the speedy end of the world. He accepted slavery, taught the subjection of wives to their husbands, the necessity of accepting the existing governments as ordained by God. He was not concerned with democracy, science, or social and political reform.

Yet to him we owe most of the significance given Jesus by Christians. His letters are the oldest documents which we have dealing with the Christian religion. Written, as some of them were, less than thirty years after the death of Jesus, they disclose to us Christian communities scattered over the Near East and even in the eastern part of Europe. Their members had accepted Jesus as the Christ and looked forward with confidence to the Day of Judgment which was in the immediate future. Paul is not primarily concerned with the teaching of Jesus. In fact, he refers only once or twice to anything that can be interpreted as such teaching. His central interest was in Jesus himself as the one who had brought the spirit of God to those who accepted him as the Christ. The Pauline philosophy, if one may so call it, was simple. The acceptance of Jesus as Christ not only assured the believer of acquittal at the coming Day of Judgment, but led to a transformation of his entire personality. He might expect resurrection from the abode of the dead by virtue of the divine spirit which had come into his life. Indeed, not infrequently Paul expresses himself in mystical terms in which the believer is identified with Christ and Jesus becomes the Lord who is the Spirit. What had happened to Jesus through the Spirit would happen to those who also had the Spirit. As participants in this experience, believers found the Spirit furnishing moral dynamics. They could grieve this Spirit, but if its impulses were followed they led to the type of life which Jesus himself had lived.

Christian communities who were thus being taught to transmute religious emotions into moral conduct must have had some accounts of the life of the Christ. This is not only implied in references made by Paul to the historical person, Jesus, but from the fact that shortly after Paul's death the churches in different parts of the Roman Empire gathered together these traditions and, possibly, pamphlets into the more or less continuous accounts which we have in the Gospels of Matthew, Mark, and Luke. In these Gospels we can trace the influence of the developing estimate of Jesus as the one through whom God was introduced into the life of Christian individuals and groups. The early Messianic pattern of the coming of the Spirit of God into Jesus at his baptism is preserved, but it is supplemented by the Hellenistic pattern of Incarnation. The Virgin Mary conceived the Messiah by the Holy Spirit. These Gospels, and even more distinctly the Fourth Gospel, are attempts to show how in certain definite conditions this historical Jesus expressed the divine life of a Messiah. Such memories as have thus been preserved gave content to the Pauline and Johannine exposition of Jesus as the giver of the Spirit and the eternal life. The historical Jesus became something more than a memory. He became a revelation of the divine. To get the full force of such a valuation of a historic life one must understand the significance of the Messianic pattern in which it was expressed.

II

It is no longer possible to question the historicity of Jesus. The Gospels, it is true, contain passages in which the faith of the early church has been read back into the accounts of his life and teaching, but the historic person Jesus is distinct. Whatever may be due to the faith of his followers presupposes a person and an actual historic situation within which he lived and taught, and whose patterns of thought he used.

The Jewish people, subjugated by Rome, looked forward to the time when they would be subjugators. Their repeated failures in attempting this deliverance, their perception of the tremendous power of their conquerors, forced them back to God. Only Yahweh could save.

That there should be some particular person to give expression to the Divine Spirit was a natural corollary. So the conception of the Messiah gradually shaped itself, as the *one whom God empowered with his own resident Spirit to save his people from their enemies, and to establish his Kingdom.* This is the constant formula for messiahship wherever it is met in the literature of Judaism. The Anointed is a Savior because God's Spirit operates through him; he is more than a prophet because he organizes a Kingdom rather than delivers a message; and he is a judge because he is a representative of God.

A supernatural element, or, more accurately, a divine

element, is thus present in messianic ideals. The reason why the definition was attached to this or that person was because he was regarded as possessing a God-given power to perform superhuman deeds, or was expected to perform superhuman deeds in the way of deliverance.

The messianic hope possessed more than political bearing, and the Messiah was more than a national figure. In the Jewish mind subjection to idolators and the miseries that came upon the nation, evidenced a demoniac kingdom fighting God's Kingdom. The struggle had not reached its crisis, for that would come only when the Messiah actually appeared and gathered his forces and conquered both men and devils. The demoniac kingdom had its regent in the form of the anti-Christ, who was in every way the opposite of the Christ. Gathering up into itself the accumulated thought of the struggle, both cosmic and moral, in which men are involved, the anti-Christ expectation was easily attached to men who had great powers of doing harm. The defeat of Satan and his representatives was to mark the transition from the present to the coming age.

This general conception was transferred to Jesus, who had appeared in the messianic succession. The reasons for this are apparent on the pages of the New Testament. In fact, the problem of the development of the messianic belief in Jesus does not seem to be as complicated as some insist. If one looks at the matter historically, here are the facts: Jesus appears announcing that the Kingdom of Heaven is at hand, and telling people to prepare for it. He then proceeds to heal demoniacs, and is regarded as having power to which the Prince of Evil has to submit. He follows up this conquest of the demoniac powers by healing the sick and further undoing the work of Satan. To understand the situation there is no need of stopping to argue whether devils actually were cast out or neurotics cured. The fact is that the people regarded Jesus, and Jesus presented himself, as the Stronger Man, able to bind the Strong Man. Further, he endeavored to make people prepare for the divine Kingdom's coming. To be so prepared was to have eternal life, i. e., to be saved in the future age. And the only complete preparation was discipleship and moral likeness to himself, the Son of Man, i. e., the type of the Kingdom.

His certainty as to the immediacy of the Kingdom, the guarantee of his own Kingdom-likeness by his power both as teacher and as healer, led men to conjecture that he was the Christ, just as they had conjectured that others were the Christ. Belief in his resurrection enabled those who held it to insist that he was in authority on high. The evidence of this authority was the work of the Holy Spirit. Those who accepted Jesus as Christ were so transformed that they were given power to resist the assault of sin through the "flesh," and to rise triumphant over death in the resurrection of the body.

That the disciples should attribute to Jesus and to his future the eschatological beliefs of the Apocalypses was unavoidable. They did not see in him a second person of a consubstantial Trinity, but they did see in him one whom God had empowered by his own resident Spirit to be the founder of his Kingdom and to save his people from Satan, sin, and death. That he actually did have such power they believed was evidenced in their own experience. They could think of him only as the expression of the saving Spirit of God in an individual.

III

The outstanding element in the character of Jesus is obviously sacrificial love. He gave men what he had to give, himself and his service. The two cannot be separated from each other. His was not a life of acquisitiveness either of material goods or of honor. He cheered those who were poor and outcast, and served them, sacrificing what must have seemed as good to them as they do to us—family fortune, friendships, comfort, life. He did not attempt to enforce his rights, nor does he seem to have been particularly concerned to have them recognized. He was more interested in giving justice than in acquiring it, and he died a victim to the enmity of those who would perpetuate their privileges at the expense of the unprivileged.

Another striking thing in the life of Jesus is that he brought personality into semi-personal or depersonalized groups. He was poor, despised, forsaken. The common people, the poor, the criminal, were his followers. He spoke his blessings to the hungry, the sorrowful, the poor. He himself partook in the struggle of these depressed classes. He gave personal value to the despised masses. He took upon himself the form of a servant and died the death of a criminal.

The contrast between his inner supremacy and his outer humiliation, however, is more apparent than real, because humiliation was his way of bringing personal values to life. Without it his life might have been interesting, but it would not have been important. It was because he recognized the worth of the human soul even in its least respected state that he has been worshiped as the savior of the world rather than of classes.

With him there was no room for bond or free, male or female, national aggressions or class consciousness. The more one studies society, the more one feels that the future will belong either to Jesus Christ or to coercive mechanism. Wherever one turns one finds the same issues dominant. Is the world to progress only by the enforced surrender of rights, or will it move forward under the inspiration of those free and Christlike spirits who are willing to share their privileges with others? Charity is only a crude expression of such an attitude, for charity may exist even while the charitable hold fast to privileges which make their almsgiving necessary. This age needs love, not charity. Power, newly acquired by those long repressed, needs moral control if it is not to become the tyranny of new privileged classes. The real hope for the future lies in the faith of those who believe that the example and spirit of Jesus are the keys to unlock social difficulties. In this day there is call for the same sort of faith as that of Athanasius who refused to believe that Jesus Christ was an illusion or a demi-god. Those who intelligently believe in the definitions of Jesus which the formulas of the great Councils set forth must transmute orthodoxy into love. They must be willing not only to make the sacrifices necessary to steady social reconstruction, but also to Christianize the process itself, making it an expression of the divine will of brotherliness seen in the example and the spiritual leadership of Jesus.

By the middle of the 19th century the historical study of the Gospels caused Jesus to step from the frame in which the theologians had placed him. Thorough-going historical method made the Jesus of the Gospels quite other than the Christ of orthodoxy, but the negative results of such study were less significant than the new interest in Jesus' teaching. At first, the interpretation of his words and ideas was undoubtedly affected by the idealism of its exponents. But even when the force of historical method convinced students that he shared views current among his contemporaries, his personality and spirit became the center of loyalty for those who were only incidentally interested in post-mortem life and very much concerned about better conditions for human life here and now. Jesus, portrayed in the New Testament, dramatized in an exemplary way religious basis for morals. To those who took him seriously, love seemed a practicable basis on which to build a human society because God is love.

Perhaps the criticism passed upon those who undertook thus to estimate the moral and religious significance of Jesus with historical honesty was justified; perhaps in their early interpretations he did become a lay figure upon which they could hang their ideals. But it cannot be denied that such treatment of Jesus has given him a position in idealistic morality that was never given him by theological presentation. He has become a disturbing element in a warring, acquisitive and pleasure-seeking world. In saying to him, "Lord, Lord," men have endeavored as intelligently as possible to see what his teaching means when applied to conditions with which he was quite unacquainted. The vanishing point of faith in him is, therefore, not Christological definition, but individual and social morality upon a religious basis. It faces human wrong-doing with courage and a conviction, born of the faith evoked by his experience and teaching, that if men are prepared to sacrifice the lesser for the greater good they can, by conformity with the cosmic law of love, carry forward personal well-being.

IV

The acceptance of Jesus Christ as the revelation of God in human life carries with it the acceptance of personality as superior to economic efficiency. Therein we meet the key to the problem of social reconstruction. Economic efficiency is born of the attempt to master material scarcity. It is measured by production, not by wants; by materials rather than human welfare. Slavery is its nadir; wage-systems its present point of achievement. Older democracy made labor a commodity and lowered costs by reducing wages. It was the things produced and not the human folks who produced that were paramount. We have outgrown these cruel theories. We see that wages must be freed from unrestricted competition if men are to be treated as men. The personal worth of men, women, and children must be the end of the production process. A standard of living that gives safety from toxic fatigue, leisure for personal development, education and play for children is the Gibraltar beyond which reduction of wages cannot go. So says the modern labor movement. So says Christianity if it be the attitude and behaviour of Jesus.

In a world of persons, progress cannot be made through impersonality. The process lying back of today's struggles has advanced in the proportion that it has yielded to the personal ideals of Jesus. Brute force has, it is true, sometimes been used to protect institutions which have resulted from spiritual ideals. Even those who loathe war have supported a war to protect the victims of anti-democratic forces. We cannot believe that the balance of gains over the tragic losses of such a war can be made permanent unless men make personal values supreme. A better future

cannot be built on military mastery. Because men believe
in Jesus, they believe that appeal to spiritual forces must
be ultimately successful. Righteous and loving men may
perish as he perished, but righteousness and love must pre-
vail. The cross is not a symbol of a defeated God. The
personality-producing activities which Jesus revealed will
ultimately end appeals to brute force in industry and
politics. Always to have recourse to brute force, whether
human or cosmic, is a denial of the God of the spiritual
order whom Christ revealed.

The urgent needs of our new social crisis will not be
given Christian satisfaction until our theology is shaped by
our new knowledge of society and of the cosmos. Chris-
tology must be social. For if we think little about "essence"
and human nature in the realistic sense which was so important to the Alexandrian theologians, we are mightily
concerned with society and the people who compose it.
Repeatedly there sweeps over us the same despair as to the
outcome of social relations which Augustine felt as to human nature. How is it ever to be possible for the world to
emerge from its present antagonisms and hatreds? How
are economic conditions ever to approach that equity
which we feel they now lack? Is human nature itself possessed of powers which merit trust? Such doubts challenge
a religious world-view. Their answers will not be born of
economic forces or biology or even ideas. Our elemental
Christian faith is as much at stake today as in the fourth
century. We no longer use Stoic *logoi* and oriental mysteries in our thinking, but we believe Jesus discloses to us
cosmic activity as a basis for the better organization of
society in the interest of the personal values of individuals.

V

Thus to take Jesus seriously is not to affirm the validity of those pre-scientific conceptions which he shared with his contemporaries. It is more than to accept the dogma as to his being the incarnation of the second person of the Trinity. It is not to raise into legislation his directions as to how those should live who expected the end of an age and the catastrophic establishment of God's Kingdom. It is not a sentimental passivity which prevents participation in social processes. It is rather the belief that in his attitudes and ideals we can see the operation of the personality-producing activities upon which human welfare must ultimately rest. It is to adopt the course of action which is dominated by his spirit. It is to believe that until that action becomes a basis for a social life we shall not see the end of poverty or of war or of those other evils which have disintegrated a social order because men and women have not regarded others as persons.

But to take him seriously does not mean that we shall look out upon humanity with myopic optimism. Jesus was not afraid to attack that which he regarded as opposed to the will of the heavenly Father. Good people must be protected from people who refuse to accept personal values as final. The road from every Jerusalem to every Jericho will have to be policed. Loyalty to such belief cannot stop with repentance. It must be led to an intelligent organization of life which can further the personality-producing activities of the universe. That such an organization is as practicable as it is difficult, and that the sacrifices which it entails are not too costly is the supreme Christian faith.

It is from this point of view that one sees the significance

of the death of Christ. The various doctrines of the Atonement are something more than some crude conception of
placating an angry deity. Each one of them attributes the
initiative in forgiveness to God. The legitimacy of the
divine forgiveness has been questioned by those for whom
the idea of justice was set by current political and judicial
practices, but it has been justified in patterns drawn from
such practices themselves. Every doctrine of the Atonement is a testimony to the significance of Jesus as introduc-
ing spiritual influences into human life. He dies rather than
question their ultimate triumph. Stripped of the patterns in
which they have been set forth, in him the personality-
producing activities of the universe find themselves chal-
lenged by the results of the lower stages through which
they have progressed. If personal values are to be furthered,
they must endure the opposition of these lower stages without recourse to violence and coercion. The cross becomes a
symbol, therefore, not of a defeated God, but of the way
in which the personality-producing activities of the universe operate. Temporary defeat is not a testimony to the
impotence of such activities. It is the sign manual of the
faith of Jesus that, despite its cost, love is a practicable
basis upon which to build a human relation because it is the
expression of cosmic activity pictured as the love of a
righteous God.

Are human beings to be treated as economic and military
commodities, or as persons? This ever repeated question is not
whether rich people and cultivated people are to be so
treated. They always have been regarded as persons. The
feudal lord, the member of a noble caste, the king, the
wealthy, have always been estimated as persons. It is the
poor, the oppressed, the sick, the slave, the criminal, who

have been depersonalized. Social evolution has been an effort to personalize them, yet at every step of the tragic struggle the powers of those who have achieved full personal rights too often have been ready to force back all others into the place of economic cogs.

Here is the ultimate question of Christian faith. Whatever may be the uncertainty relative to various details, however much the Gospel picture may have been colored by the beliefs of the early church, does the Jesus of the Gospels, in his life and teachings, represent the way in which the personality-producing activities of the universe can find expression in an individual reacting to a social situation? Over against the affirmation of such a faith lies the denial of love as a practicable basis for human relations. Opposition to Christ becomes more than a question of dogma. It is a declaration of disbelief in the personal rights of the individual and of reliance upon coercion as justifiable agents by those who can exercise it. There can be no compromise with a view that regards the ideals of Jesus as wishful weakness or with that which justifies the coercion of those who cannot resist. To restrict the significance of Christianity to preparation for post mortem happiness by those subservient to the will of their masters is a denial of Jesus as an interpreter of cosmic activity in the life of the individual.

Chapter VII

THEISM MORE THAN ITS PATTERNS

Our discussion leads to the recognition of two views of God. The first is that of an infinite spirit who exists apart from the universe, but whose will may be affected by prayer. As a sovereign he rules a rebellious world, but will give eternal felicity to those whom he selects and enables to take advantage of the atoning death of Christ. As a Father, he is loving and despite all the misfortunes which fall upon humanity, may be trusted to give worthy gifts to his children. It is this pattern-God who is judged *emeritus* by those who take a realistic view of man's relation to the universe given by science.

According to the other view, the term God is not existential but symbolical. Human life is seen to be the outcome of and dependent upon the personality-producing activities of the universe, and the term God enables men to use experience gained in the relation of human persons, both individually and socially, as means of reciprocal adjustment to such cosmic activity.

The contrast between these two conceptions is much like that between conceptions of man's relationship to natural forces. Men once looked upon them as sufficiently distinct to be treated as separate entities. The stars seemed to be living beings, fire, lightning, storms, rivers, powers of reproduction in plant and animal life, were treated as superhuman personalities to be feared and placated. As knowledge grew, there came to be recognized what are called natural laws. These, when understood, enabled scientists to extend the frontier of knowledge and discover new elements in the cosmic environment. The same developments are to be seen in religions whose adherents have accepted the scientific interpretation of nature. They too have seen in the universe activities which cannot be understood as actions of superhuman personalities. With them there must be adjustment and cooperation if human welfare is to be advanced. Cosmic law is as traceable in humanity as in the movements of the heavenly bodies. Adjustment to those aspects of cosmic activity which have given rise to human beings is furthered by such individual relations and social institutions as increase personal values. Individuals in growing personal through social relations express the personality-producing activities of the universe from which they have emerged.

It is from this point of view that we can examine different religious systems. To understand them we must look behind doctrines and practices. By them, men of different social orders have sought to further adjustment with those cosmic activities with which they more or less unconsciously feel personally related. The characteristics of the Christian religion lie in its techniques of bringing this adjustment to pass. As in every religion, they are relative to the social order from which they sprang.

I

What, then, is this subliminal Christianity in which man may believe while he rejects the formulas of orthodoxy and the authority of the church? It is not to be described by a denial of such doctrines or authority, but as a complex of values which various Christian groups and institutions seek to put at the service of mankind. In these basic values dramatized in Jesus the Christian church throws down its challenge to every type of mechanistic interpretation of life and every attempt to reduce a world of men to self-indulgent brutes. These values are what the doctrinal patterns of all theologies have attempted to make acceptable in successive grades of human culture. If they are true, they are invaluable aids to better and more hopeful living.

1. The cosmos is not mechanistic, but instinct with personality-producing activity—forces which have had a part in the evolution of humanity and must be treated as elements in the environment in which men must live. That is what Christianity means when it says that there is a God in whom we live and move and have our being. For the word *God* is the term used to describe the personality-producing activities of the cosmos.

2. Christianity's God of law is a God of love. This is the heart of the teaching of Jesus and it is this which every theological system has endeavored to make tenable and helpful. If difficulty in holding this belief sprang from casting the relation of God and man in political analogies, it was met by corollaries drawn from the same patterns, and God's Son, Jesus Christ, was regarded as bearing the punishment which otherwise would have fallen upon humanity.

To a considerable degree, these religious patterns have been outgrown. Cosmic activity is more than a sovereign, but the problem of evil is still with us. The reply of the Christian involves no denial of suffering or wrongdoing. He believes that as men grow in knowledge they will better understand cosmic forces and learn how to control or to adjust themselves to them.

But he also believes that there are activities which will cooperate in this endeavor of mankind to live superior to mechanism. The same activities that have made us personal will aid us in our attempts to be more personal. Christianity does not undertake to decide why we have such a universe as we have, but it does show how men can live superior to all the mechanisms which they have inherited and gain help from personality-evolving activities of the universe.

3. Personal values are superior to all others. It is this conviction that dignifies the more or less misdirected zeal of ascetics and Puritans. The effort to express this conviction in actual social relations has varied with the intelligence and the social structure of different periods. One could not expect a society whose very existence depended upon the maintenance of feudal institutions to be democratic.

But the Christian church struggled with the crudities and brutalities of men who were only with difficulty raising themselves from barbarism, showed that humanity had worth, and offered Heaven to the poor as well as to the rich. We see more clearly the enemies of the evaluation of men as persons, and although we are not yet sufficiently intelligent to know just how to restrain crime and unscrupulous acquisitiveness, we are inspired by this same conviction: Men are persons and not machines.

4. Human progress follows the democratizing of privilege. This is the meaning of love as Christ taught and embodied it. For love is more than sentimentality; it is the expression of the cosmic process of coordination and in-

tegration on the level of personality. For this reason Christian idealism has always opposed force, although Christians have been so unenlightened as sometimes to try to achieve their ends by force. In the effort to give rather than to get justice, the Christian religion has been immensely aided by having its ideal dramatized in the life and death of its founder. The loyalty of Christians to him will be measured by their endeavor to reproduce in their world-order the same attitude which he embodied in his. Goodwill will thus furnish the motive, and science the technique of a new stage in social evolution.

5. Kindliness and service assure help-gaining adjustment with the personality-producing activities of the universe. Such a fact can be expressed in human analogies of father and son so characteristic of Jesus' teaching. But the truth is independent of the particular analogy. The Christian religion may use anthropomorphic analogies, but the relationship itself is more than anthropomorphism. Whoever can accept evolution as the most likely hypothesis by which to organize our knowledge of the emergence of humanity will recognize the inevitability of this Christian position. Instead of seeking a de-individualized union with a static Brahma, it looks toward and develops a more personal individual because of adjustment with and appropriation of the personality-producing activities of the universe. That there are such activities cannot be denied without denying human nature itself. It is a characteristic of the mechanistic world-view that in losing its God it loses human personality.

6. To such development death is an episode, not an end. We can abandon pictures of Heaven, Hell, and Purgatory,

and yet see that they were endeavors to set forth a profound probability. An individual person whose center of life is beyond the control of the animal survivals and who is at one with the personality-producing activities of the cosmos may expect some new and less animal mode of life as the next step in evolution. Beyond such a general statement, we must be content with agnosticism tempered by hopeful analogy. But intellectual self-respect demands that we recognize that neither the New Testament nor modern Christian thinking expects the resuscitation of our animal bodies. Whatever may be the mode of life beyond death, it certainly will not be dependent upon the vestiges of the non-human past from which humanity has emerged. Death sees to that.

II

It will doubtless be objected to such an estimate of the Christian religion that it is not the sort of religion professed by millions of men and women. In reply, it can be said with equal truth, that traditional Christianity has not prevented the present world-wide tragedy and that there are an increasing number of persons to whom the anthropomorphisms and group practices of the churches make little appeal. If Christianity is to have any part in the development of the spiritual life of such persons, it must be shown to be something more than a projection of group practices and beliefs. To hold that a line of conduct is in accordance with the will of God which is itself a projection of social idealism undoubtedly has an emotional efficiency. To turn to a sovereign God when humanity is weak will always be a source of comfort for those who are defeated. But it may also be an excuse for refusal to act in ways which involve sacrifice. The God of the church has too often been the God of the privileged classes. It is only too easy to thrust upon him responsibilities which ought to be borne intelligently by men and women.

It would be unjust to deprive mankind of the religious satisfactions which come from uncritical reliance upon conventional theism. Such a course of action would be farthest from the purpose of those who feel that there is some deeper basis on which to ground the confidence that love is a practicable basis on which to build human relations. For such persons, whose thought is forced by scientific method to discover values that lie beneath the developing idea of God, there remains the reliance upon the understanding of man's relationship with cosmic activity. To feel that the ideals which Christianity sets forth as the contribution of Jesus are something more than wishful thinking or sentimentality is to give religion an indisputable position in human life. To feel that sacrifice in the interest of enriched personal living of others is not camouflaged defeatism is stabilized by reliance upon the personality-producing activities of the universe. Conduct which seeks to develop personal values is seen to be not only an acceptance of the universe but a projection of those activities into and through human relations. It promises no miracle, nor indeed expects one. It realizes that intelligence is as necessary in such cooperative adjustment as in the discovery and utilization of chemical and physical forces. Religion becomes conformity and help-gaining adjustment with cosmic activity. With such adjustment there comes new strength and confidence that human beings will not be comrades in doom if only they will be comrades in the cooperative extension of cosmic activity through social organization.

In so far as God represents the personality-producing activities of the universe, he ceases to be identified with any anthropomorphic pattern in which such activities have been portrayed. He is not lost in the shadows of a dialectic that declares him to be undefinable. He represents no absentee sovereignty, nor a personality who may be swayed by human petition or held responsible for human wrongdoing. His will is not mysterious, but a symbol of an orderly process in the universe with which man must establish reciprocal adjustment if personal welfare is to be advanced. The dogmas and practices which have become sacred by their very age have efficiency in so far as they aid this adjustment. Intelligent action in the furtherance of personal values is seen to be more imperative than prayers for mercy from a God whose ways are past finding out. The spirit and example of Jesus in his services to his own day become a guide to the sort of conduct which is in accordance with the cosmic activity. The sufferings that follow the distortion of scientific technique for the service of impersonal ends vindicate the faith which he inspired. Whether or not one uses the term *God* is no test of his religious life. That lies in his acceptance of the inevitableness of the results which follow adjustment with, or hostility to, the cosmic activities which Jesus, in Jewish patterns, expressed. But, for those who find their religious life stimulated by the use of the term *God* as an aid to their individual and social adjustment to the personality-producing activities of the universe, there can be no question of his presence. Religious faith becomes a warning against all reliance upon force, however organized by science, and a courage-breeding assurance that love is a practicable basis upon which to build human relations since it is an expression in human relations of cosmic activity. As the symbol of such activity, God is *not* emeritus.

DATE DUE
